To: Eileen

With Best Wishes,

Will Marshall

RICH SHAREOWNER,

POOR SHAREOWNER! ™

RICH SHAREOWNER,
POOR SHAREOWNER! ™

COMMON SENSE
FOR
INVESTORS
AND
MANAGERS!

Will Marshall

Writer's Showcase
San Jose New York Lincoln Shanghai

Rich Shareowner, Poor Shareowner! ™
Common Sense for Investors and Managers!

All Rights Reserved © 2002 by William G. Marshall

Excerpts from *The Wisdom of the Native Americans* by Kent Nerburn are reprinted with the permission of New World Library.
www.newworldlibrary.com.

Writer's Showcase
an imprint of iUniverse, Inc.

For information address:
iUniverse, Inc.
5220 S. 16th St., Suite 200
Lincoln, NE 68512
www.iuniverse.com

ISBN: 0-595-21789-3

Printed in the United States of America

For

Marianne

Contents

Acknowledgements

Thank you for buying and reading this book!......I hope that you will find a quiet spot to relax and enjoy the story, while at the same time finding the ideas enlightening, thought provoking and at times, disconcerting.

You will recognize that this book is a product of many life experiences. I would like to acknowledge some of the many people who influenced it.

First, to my wife and daughter, I give my thanks for their selfless support during my career, the examples of character that they demonstrate everyday, and the encouragement to write this book.

My mother, father and a tree farm in Western Pennsylvania taught me the importance of hard work and character. They also taught me that all honest work is honorable, and that everyone deserves an equal chance.......A Pennsylvania Bell Telephone lineman, by the name of Dick McCain, volunteered countless hours and cold nights in canoes and tents as he cajoled and motivated a handful of young Boy Scouts to achieve Eagle Scout rank. He knew, but never said, that he was teaching us the values of a lifetime.......Lehigh University taught me how to think, and at Pensacola, Marine D. I., Gunnery Sergeant Bodine taught the meaning of mind over body.

The use of a dude ranch setting was the product of wonderful summer experiences with my family and many new friends at Rainbow Trout Ranch in Colorado's San Juan Mountains. Doug and Linda Van Berkum along with their son David, his wife Jane (who can ride and rope with the best even while pregnant!), the ranch hands, and cowboy singer Will Dudley, deserve our thanks for keeping many of the best traditions of the West alive.

During my 20 years at Nalco Chemical Company, I was privileged to work with people who collectively were of the highest caliber. They tried to do the best that they knew for the company's constituents, and that included the public and the environment.

The practical side of finance and corporate governance is too often learned through trial and error. I am grateful to many people who put me to the test, and corrected my errors. I am thankful for bankers like Deborah Stevens, Bob Bourke, Wendy Gorman, Bob Ragland, Jeff Hines, Geoff Stringer and Dennis Neumann who did their level best to help their customer create value.......There were others.......I am also exceptionally grateful to the many people in finance at Nalco who have supported me over the years! I especially want to recognize those who have been principals in challenging me with the toughest questions: Manuel Diaz, Mary deJonge, Stan Gibson, Glen Haeflinger, Frederic Jung, Steve Landsman, Gerard Lamarche, Gilberto Pinzon, Sergio Sousa, Judy Sprieser and Gina Tuggle. Along with many of these people, Dick Murphy provided comments that made this book better.

But, this book would not have been written without the questioning, example and inspiration provided by Liz Ewing, my successor as Treasurer of Nalco. During the five years we worked together, Liz's questions challenged me to think about and to see the need to explain in plain English the core issues of creating Shareowner Value.......In the process of doing my job, I learned from the standards and examples that she set in human relationships everyday.......And in doing her job, she demonstrated a level of integrity second to none.

My thanks to all of you—named or unnamed who have been part of this effort!

Will Marshall
Hawthorn Woods, Illinois
February 2002

Preface

"Perhaps the sentiments contained in the following pages,
are not yet sufficiently fashionable to procure them general favor;
*a long habit of not thinking a thing **wrong**,*
*gives it a superficial appearance of being **right**,*
and raises at first a formidable outcry in defence of custom.
But the tumult soon subsides.
Time makes more converts than reason."
Thomas Paine
Common Sense...1776

Thus began Thomas Paine's pamphlet *Common Sense*. First appearing in print, January 10, 1776, *Common Sense* was the primary catalyst uniting American colonists to throw off English chains preventing them from realizing their freedom and economic potential.

Today, democratic, free enterprise faces a similar limitation in realizing its potential.......But, the limitation is not an external restraint imposed upon it. Rather it is a constraint imposed from within...........
.........We are captive to the popular delusion that accounting measures economic value, *and* chained to the idea that companies create economic value using principles different from those used by individuals in their personal lives.

Neither of these beliefs is true!..................This book will dispel these fictions for the reader!....And, in the process, help the reader to become a 'Richer Shareowner'!

Free enterprise is one of mankind's greatest liberators! It gives individuals the maximum opportunity to realize his or her economic potential and to freely express choice across the broadest array of alternatives.......But,...as with all human systems,...free enterprise has inefficiencies....One of free enterprise's greatest inefficiencies is that very few people understand how individuals and organizations use it to create economic value. As a result, investors ('Shareowners') corporate directors ('Boards'), officers, managers, employees and government regulators make decisions daily which inhibit creation, and in fact destroy, the very value which free enterprise empowers them to create.......We have made quantum leaps in perfecting management techniques, accounting standards, and corporate financial theory, *but* **in our exhilaration over the details of our discoveries, we have become lost in the minutia; we have forgotten what we were trying to do!......We were trying to find ways to be more effective in creating economic value!.......*Creating economic value is an applied science!*.......*To apply it, people have to understand it!***...........I hope that the common sense in this book, and the way the book has been written will help more people to understand how to measure and create economic value.

This book boils down the theory and practice of creating economic value into succinct, useable information and presents it in plain English so that individual investors and managers can understand and apply it. As ideas are boiled down and integrated, it will become clear that accounting is not the sought after 'Philosopher's Stone' for turning lead into gold. In fact for many investors and employees, accounting – especially related to acquisitions—is being used knowingly and unknowingly to turn gold into lead—destroying value for all of us!......It will also become clear that the way a company creates economic value is not mystical. It creates value the same way that we do in our personal lives.......**A company creates economic value *only* if it earns more on an investment than the cost of the money it invests.....Accounting statements don't measure this, and managers don't manage to this!**

This book attempts to have fun and to gain perspective by taking a breath,......and stepping back from the details of corporate finance theory and accounting standards. In this context, it takes sage counsel from three wise people.......The first was a Cherokee Medicine Man who said, 'We have learned too much today, so much that we have forgotten the important lessons of life.'............The second piece of wise counsel comes from Aristotle who in his *Nicomachean Ethics* shared one of life's important lessons, '....an educated person will expect accuracy in each subject only so far as the nature of the subject allows.'......And finally, Peter Drucker, the dean of management thinkers wrote a book titled *The Effective Executive* which in paraphrase said, 'To be effective in creating value, it is more important to do the right thing than to do things right.'

If a simple majority of investors and companies applied the ideas in this book, our economy would see a surge in productivity and economic value rivaling that generated by the personal computer, the Internet and the Quality Process *combined!*......*But, the reason would be different!*......The ideas in this book focus and pay people to do the right things, whereas, the PC, the Internet and the Quality Process focused people on doing things more efficiently (a.k.a. 'doing things right').......*There is a big difference between doing things right and doing the right things!*

This book has no ambitions to present new corporate finance theory, or to challenge existing theory. The ideas in this book are not academically precise,......*but*, they are directionally accurate and presented so that people can use them to create value. The goal is to give the reader the ability to get 95% of the value of the existing theory and practice with 5% of the effort.....something that we are *not* now doing as a society! Further, the goal is to attract a broad audience, and to give that audience tools to judge whether their actions or other people's actions are creating economic value!

Time is passing, and we are consuming resources belonging to future generations!......As a society, we will all be better off if we are more effective at creating economic value and less prone to destroying it! To do that, we must become more effective in identifying the right things to do!

There is one other important point to be made. While this book is about creating economic value, society creates and benefits from many other values. **The most important value we create is the character that we engender in our people—especially in our young people!** *Character is the value that gives possibility and meaning to all of the others.* **Without character, even the 'best' leadership is suspect, and the economic value we create will be abused.**

It has been said that those who don't learn from history are doomed to repeat it. This book represents 'a view from the saddle' based upon 27 years of corporate management and finance experience, benefited by reflection on how economic value has been created and destroyed in many companies. The saddle teaches that running cows in circles doesn't get them to 'trail's end'! Running cattle in circles only causes the cows to loose weight, and the cowhand to get a sore back and a thin wallet!......I hope that this book will help readers to stop running their companies, and their portfolios in circles.......I hope that greater understanding will create more value for all of a company's constituents, but principally the Shareowner, who in the process of risking his or her hard earned money to make a profit, enables the rest of us to earn a living!

1.

The Search

Once there was a bright, young woman who wanted to be successful investing in stocks.

She wanted to do this in order to be secure and independent.

Her search had taken her to the best business schools to study the theory of stock market behavior, and to the best seminars to listen to concepts of creating shareholder value.

She had traveled to London, New York, Hong Kong, Singapore, Tokyo and Omaha seeking insight into picking and trading stocks.

She had even given up part of her youth working in the mergers and acquisition department of a major investment bank trying to learn what $100 million a year investment bankers, company CEO's and Boards of Directors knew about buying and selling companies that she didn't.

It all seemed futile!

In spite of investing using the 'best' equity analysts, the 'best' brokers, the 'best' performing mutual fund managers, and following the advice of the 'best' merger and acquisition ('M&A') specialists, she felt that she wasn't any more successful and didn't understand any more about what created shareholder—or was it shareowner—value than when she began her quest 16 years ago.......

......And, she didn't feel much richer!

2.

The <u>ST</u> Ranch

It was sublime,......feeling the warmth of the sun on her shoulders yielding to the teasing coolness of the fleeting shadows of passing Aspen,...and the wisps of wind caressing her face—filling her lungs with the warm, sweet aroma of mountain pine.

As her silver BMW convertible slithered along the rugged gravel road winding higher into the San Juan Mountains, Wendy daydreamed that even though this was her first trip, Southern Colorado couldn't be more perfect than it was just now. She needed this vacation in the worst way. Six by 16 hour weeks for the past 10 months with only a short Christmas break, and the irrational behavior of her stocks had worn her down. As she approached 8,000 feet in altitude, she had the exquisite feeling of the tension being physically drawn from her nerves, muscles and mind as it evaporated into the clear, mountain air, ...or, then again, maybe she was just getting the altitude sickness she had been warned about.

Either way, Wendy was beginning to feel invigorated as she turned in to the ST Bar Ranch road which would climb the final distance to the dude ranch Lodge at an altitude of 9,000 feet. Wendy had heard stories of the Ranch from friends back East who had stayed here. She was excited to try something really new this vacation even though she was concerned that it might be a shade more rustic than she would normally like. As the ranch road wound through the Aspen and Ponderosa Pine, the scenery gradually gave way to a view of the large pine Lodge seated on a shoulder of the mountainside. About two hundred feet back in the pines on the same flat, fourteen small log cabins were discretely situated, each capable of holding about 5 to 7 people. For the next week Wendy would have one of the cabins to herself as well as one of the horses which she could see pastured beside a cool looking trout stream about 1,000 feet down the mountain. Not too far from the stream, she could also see a small barn and bunkhouse for the ranch hands.

At 3:30 on Sunday afternoon, the small twelve-car parking lot was almost full with the week's new arrivals. A Lexus LX 470, Suburban, Excursion, Tahoe and Camry with license plates from California, Texas, Massachusetts, Michigan and Illinois were all represented, as well as rental cars with Colorado and New Mexico plates. The rentals had undoubtedly come from the airports at Albuquerque, Denver or Colorado Springs.

Several humming birds sipped sweet water from feeders as she stepped onto the Lodge's 20-foot deep, roofed porch. It wrapped around the east and south side of the Lodge and overlooked the pastures and valley below. The oversized wood chairs looked like a wonderful place to enjoy coffee and watch the morning sunrise.

Wendy's next step was simultaneously intimidating, awesome and thrilling. She crossed the threshold of the main entrance into the Lodge's Great Room. If the size of the room didn't take her breath, then the untamed wildness of the animals and romance of the western furnishings and tack did!......Growling bear, stalking bobcats and a fanged cougar surveyed moose, antelope and deer on the 14-foot high log sidewalls. Below them at shoulder level, ancient, worn saddles, lariats and guns hung as if ready for tomorrow's ride. It was daunting to imagine comparing her riding skills to those of the people who had broken in these saddles! From the 40-foot high, sloped ceiling hung chandeliers made of shed elk horn, and throughout the 40 by 80 foot room, comfortable looking stuffed chairs and sofas overflowed with pillows containing cowboy and western scenes. At the far end of the room a great stone fireplace capable of burning 8-foot logs stood a kindly watch.

"Howdy and welcome to the ST Bar Ranch!" said a friendly voice. "My name is Jan Wilmoth. I manage the greeting, cooking and cleaning side of the ranch! My guess is that you're Wendy Stevens! Right?"

Wendy reached for Jan's extended hand, "That's right, and I am looking forward to spending an exciting week with you!"

"You can count on it!" replied Jan. "Let me show you to your cabin so that you can settle in. We'll all get together at 6:15 for supper, and we'll introduce everybody including the ranch hands."

Jan escorted Wendy to cabin 7 named the 'Philosopher's Stone.' While old, the cabin was 'Spic and Span' clean. It had a small sitting porch, two bedrooms with closets and a bathroom with hot and cold running water. Wendy unpacked her bags, sat down in the big, over-stuffed, bedroom chair and promptly fell asleep, as the altitude had tired her out.

On her watch it was 7:30 p.m. Wendy quickly wakened, disturbed at herself for missing supper and the introductions. Almost as quickly, she felt relief as she remembered that her watch was still on Eastern Time; it was only 5:30 here in the Eastern Rockies. She freshened up and walked down to the Lodge.

Wendy wasn't sure what to expect about the people to be met when she entered the Lodge. What she found relieved her! She wasn't the only one who had a bit to learn about ranch life this week. While they were still straggling in, the guests were mostly family groups of three to six with children ranging from 5 to young adult. They wore jeans and L.L. Bean flannel shirts or sweaters to protect against the cool evening breeze. A few had clearly come to the mountains to fish rather than to ride, and they looked quite at home in their good fitting Orvis trout fishing garb. One handsome fisherman, named Tim, a dentist from Michigan, especially caught her eye, but as she learned later that evening, he had already been happily netted and was here with his family. The guests were an eclectic collection of professionals, executives and entrepreneurs from every region of the states, and Wendy thought that would make for some good supper and trail conversations.

As the supper bell sounded outside for the second time, two sets of great doors on either side of the fireplace opened, and the 60 guests together with 15 or so assembled ranch staff filed into another 40 x 100 foot room. This Dining Room was filled with 16 tables each surrounded by 8 seats. At least one ranch staffer sat at each table along with an entire family. By the end of the week, this changed with tables being formed by the different age groups of children, and the adults mixing seats together from one meal to the next.

Wendy sat at a table in the center of the room with Debra Morgan, a Northwestern University Business School professor, Debra's husband, John, who was an attorney, and their three teenage children. They were joined by two of the wranglers, "Dakota" and Glen. You could tell the wranglers; except for one older man at the first row table by the fireplace, they never took off their cowboy hats except for funerals and when they sat down inside at a supper table.

The ranch staff was a curious mixture of 30 young people from all over the US divided about equally between men and women. There were a few married couples. Just about all of the staff was in some stage of college—although some were 29 years old and still at it. About 8 of them had serious working ranch experience. They formed the core of the wranglers and were complimented by another 8 or so riders who in their spare time either rode competitively in rodeos or in English hunting or jumping competition. The rest of the staff had key duties in cooking, cabin care, children's activities or maintenance.

During supper, Debra shared her excitement about this being her first trip to a ranch, and that she was looking forward to quiet time to develop some new ideas about how 'shareholder' value was created.

"Not more theories!" thought Wendy.

Being a good guest, however, Wendy expressed interest in learning more about Debra's work during the week, and then changed the subject. She asked Dakota for his background, and what he did here. He explained that he had worked at the <u>ST</u> for ten years and was the ST Bar's Head Wrangler, responsible for the 120-horse remuda. Born and raised on a small ranch in western South Dakota near Belle Fourche, he began riding when he was 4 years old, and loved working outdoors with horses. Then he said, "Now Chisholm over there is the Ramrod for the cattle you will be pushing this week. Chisholm is from Texas, and was suckled by a mama longhorn. He can tell you anything you want to know about them ornery critters."

Debra jumped in with a question, "You are responsible for the horses, Chisholm has the cattle, and Jan handles the office. Who owns the Ranch?"

"We don't know," said Glen, "and it doesn't really matter. Whoever it is picked a good bunch to work with, and the paycheck is always on time and fair."

"But who runs the ranch?" persisted Debra.

"We all do!" said Dakota. "But, when we have a tough problem, we go to Sam. He thinks like an owner, even though he gets a payday just like the rest of us."

"Who's Sam?" asked Debra's husband, John.

"Sam's the older fellow over there at the center table in the first row. He's wearing the red, brush-popper shirt with black and green stripes. He's a helluva hand in spite of being from back east."

Before John could ask his next question, Sam rose with his back to the Dining Room fireplace and tapped his glass with his knife.

The room became silent.

Sam spoke in a sure, loud voice. "Ladies, gentlemen, girls and boys, we welcome you to the ST Bar Ranch. We know that you came for good fun and a memorable experience. It's our pleasure to help you have them. My name is Sam McAllen. I'll serve as the Chief Host while you are here. In a moment Jan Wilmoth, who you met on arrival, Dakota Smith, Head Wrangler, and John Chisholm, Ramrod, will introduce the <u>ST</u> hands and tell you about the week's activities. After that, we ask that each of you take turns standing and introducing yourself to us."

Sam continued, "Ranching is more than riding horses, eating dust and chasing cattle. It is a way of thinking, working and living. We hope that you take some of it home with you. During the week, feel free to ask questions or to let us know of any needs. We want you to enjoy your stay so that you will come back."

Sam introduced Jan and sat down.

Wendy was impressed. While she hadn't learned much about Sam in a biographical sense, his direct, yet warm manner of speech, his straight posture and open gestures, and his eye contact indicated a lot about the man and the sincerity of his words. She also sensed that he had depth and experience well beyond ranching. As people introduced themselves, she thought that it would be worthwhile to meet Sam and to learn more about him.

She got the opportunity later that evening.

PART I

Shaking Out The Loop!

3.

Why Do People Invest?

It was 8 p.m. when supper broke up. During the briefing Wendy learned that she would be riding with Debra's family tomorrow, as well as with Tom and Georgia Roman, a husband and wife long distance trucking team from Washington state and a stock broker, Jim Perrier, his wife, Patty and their three children from Atlanta. Gina Evans would be their wrangler.

Small groups were forming in the Great Room. Wendy filled her coffee mug and walked over to four adults who had gathered around Sam. Nancy Patterson, a Chemical Engineer in sales, was trying to learn more about Sam. She certainly knew the art of asking probing questions! Between Nancy and Georgia, the no holds barred, better half of the trucking team, they had learned that Sam had come to the Ranch about 10 years ago to enjoy the clear air, plain talk and hard, yet rewarding physical side of ranching. They also learned that prior to coming to Colorado, Sam had been a senior financial officer at a sizeable company, and had developed some thoughts on how money is made and lost for shareowners.

"That's great!" said Debra who had just joined the group. "I'm writing a paper explaining some different approaches to creating 'shareholder' value, and I'd like to compare my ideas with yours."

"I would like to hear your ideas too, Sam!" said Wendy. "I hope that your search to discover how to make money in the stock market has been more successful than mine!"

"Me too!" said Georgia. "Tom and I are constantly listening to business radio in the rig, and we use our wireless to trade for our retirement account."

"I always want to please guests!" said Sam.......'But, you need to understand that the ideas I will share with you are nothing more than common sense, and will provide insight into both the Shareowner and manager's roles in creating value for the Shareowner."

"All the better!" said Debra. "Where do we start?"

"Well......." said Sam, encouraging the small group to sit in the comfortable ranch chairs. "Let's start at the beginning.......When you are driving cattle, the two most important things to know at the beginning of the trail are how to use your equipment and where the trail is supposed to end!.........So, let's begin by shaking the loop out on our rope and ask the 'trail's end' question about investing........Why do people invest?"

There was an uncomfortable silence.

Sam's eyes twinkled. "You know, last week I phrased the question a little differently. I asked, 'Why do people own stock?'.......A cute, little, six-year-old from Wyoming gave me the answer. She said, 'Because they have pretty, brown eyes.'"

He grinned.........'I couldn't disagree!......Some stock you just have to love, because you sure don't make money on them!"

The group laughed and relaxed. Sam repeated the question, "**Why do people invest?**"

There was an additional pause, and then Georgia spoke up.

"I don't know the theory, but I know why I own stock!" said Georgia. "I own stock to put more cash in my pocket!"

There was a stunned silence.......It was almost as if Georgia's answer was too direct,......too simple!

Sam sat quietly, surveying the guests' faces.

Finally, with a smile on his face, Sam said, "Bull's-eye, Georgia! Shareowners invest to have more cash in their pockets.......They may want the cash to save for retirement, for a child's education, or to buy a new car,......but at the end of the day, **we all invest to have more cash in our pockets;......to be able to buy more!**"

"Why do people invest?"

"People invest to have more cash in their pockets;
To be able to buy more!"

4.

What is Cash?

"Georgia, what do you mean by 'cash'?" asked Sam.

"Well," she paused thinking, "In an investing sense, cash is what I have in my money market account, plus the value of my stock, because when I sell my stock, the cash is put into my money market account."

"Georgia, that's a great answer! We're going to learn a lot from you!" encouraged Sam.

Georgia blushed.

"Georgia, when you say value of your stock, I assume that you mean the **Market Value**[1] which in this case **is the number of shares that you own times the current market price per share**. Is that right?" asked Sam.

"That's right!" she responded.

Looking at the rest of the group, Sam continued, "Georgia's *portfolio* consists of cash in her money market account plus the Market Value of

---

1. Throughout this book, the term Market Value is used either in the context of (1) the Market Value of the shares owned by a specific Shareowner (i.e. Market Value = number of shares owned by the Shareowner x current market price per share), *or* (2) the Market Value of the entire company (i.e. Market Value = total number of shares outstanding x current market price per share.)

the stock she owns. Let's use the term 'Cash Value' to represent the total value of her portfolio........We'll also assume that the Market Value of her stock really is the cash we can get for it when we sell it. Sometimes that's a big assumption because just like in the cattle business, the price for stock (or cattle) can change a lot between the time you start the cattle to market and the time you get them there!"

"But let's refine our definition of cash with one last question......**Suppose that Georgia and Tom had borrowed money to buy stock. Would that change the definition of Cash Value?**"

"Yes!" said Wendy, drawing on her knowledge of merger and acquisitions analysis. "**The debt eventually has to be paid back using cash in the portfolio. So, the** *definition of the Cash Value of a Shareowner's portfolio* **becomes** *the sum* **of cash in the money market account** *plus* **the Market Value of my stock** *minus* **the debt in the Shareowner's portfolio.**"

"This is a very knowledgeable group!" exclaimed Sam. "We will define the Cash Value of a Shareowner's portfolio, exactly as Wendy just described it."

*The Definition of the Cash Value
of an Investment Portfolio:*

Cash Value	=	Cash in the Money Market Account	+	Market Value of Stock	-	*Shareowner's Debt in the Portfolio*

5.

How do Real People define Shareowner Value?

Sam continued, "Nancy or Tom, how about your thoughts on the next question?"

"When I own a company's stock, I have been told that I want someone to create Shareowner Value for me. But, I have heard many conflicting definitions of Shareowner Value.......I'm confused! **What does Shareowner Value mean?**"

Tom responded, "**As a Shareowner, the only value a stock has to me is the cash it puts into my pocket. So, the value of a share is its Market Value;......the same Market Value** which we just used in the definition of Cash Value."

"That's right!" said Debra's husband, John. "When I look at our retirement money, I don't look at the P/E (price to earnings) ratio or some other accounting number, I just want to see the total Cash Value of our portfolio."

"Makes sense!" said Steve.......'"The only way a Shareowner can realize his objective of having more cash to spend is to sell the stock at its current market price, which, hopefully, is above the price that he paid for it. The accounting numbers are merely ink on paper and don't translate to hard, cold cash unless they are reflected in the stock's price."

No one else commented, so Sam said, "Tom, it looks like you've come up with a definition of Shareowner Value that real people can relate to!.......*At a point in time*, **Shareowner Value equals the Market Value of the stock.**"

Georgia gave Tom a high five, and the group cheered his success!

Shareowner Value Defined:

At a given point in time, Shareowner Value is defined as follows:

Shareowner Value	=	Market Value of Stock

6.

The Creation of Shareowner Value isn't the same for Everyone!

John spoke next, "Wait Sam, I need some help! Debra's professor friends, often use the term 'creation (or destruction) of Shareowner Value', and they appear to use it in different ways. What does it mean?"

"Let me try that!" said Nancy.

"Glad to have the help!" replied Sam.

Nancy began. "Like Georgia, I don't know financial theory, but based upon our definition of Shareowner Value as the Market Value of a stock, I think that *over a period of time*, Shareowner Value is created if the stock price goes up, and value is destroyed when the stock price goes down!......To pick up on Steve's point, even if accounting earnings are going up, if the stock's price goes down, the Cash Value of my stock is being destroyed."

"Yeah!" said Tom, "The difference in the Market Value of my stock over time tells me the amount of Cash Value that the stock has created or destroyed for me."

"I think that we need to add dividends." interjected Wendy. "In other words, over the period of time that you own the stock, the company will probably pay cash dividends, and you will put the cash into your portfolio's money market account. Those dividends will earn interest..........So, *over the time that you own the stock,* the creation (or destruction) of value is the change in Market Value of the stock *plus* the cash dividends which it pays, *together with* any earnings on the dividends."

"Excellent addition, Wendy!" observed Sam as he scribbled down what they had said on a piece of paper.

Shareowner Value Creation (Destruction)	=	Cash Paid In Dividends (plus any earnings on that cash)	+	Increase (Decrease) in Market Value of Stock

"Sam paused, then pointing to the piece of paper, he asked, "*Is the creation (or destruction) of Shareowner Value the same for all Shareowners?*"

"*Yes,*" said Debra. In any given period of time, the stock price changes the same amount for all of the Shareholders, and the dividend paid on each share is the same."

"*Debra, I have to disagree!*" said Georgia. "The stock only creates value for me if I sell it for more than I bought it. But, Wendy is right, I also need to include any dividends received while I owned the stock as well as interest that I earn on the dividends."

After an awkward 30 second silence, John said, "It sounds to me like you're both right! **The amount of creation or destruction of Shareowner Value *depends on* whether we are looking at the *group of Shareowners* between time A and time B, *or* whether we are looking at *an individual Shareowner* during the time that he or she owns the stock.**"

................Silence!............

With a wry smile on his face, Sam spoke, "John!......More than you will ever know, it pains me to admit, that *an attorney*—YOU!—has identified the key source of confusion for Shareowners, Boards, managers and academics that try to understand the process of creating Shareowner Value!"......

John smiled quizzically at the compliment.

Sam continued soberly,......"It makes a **BIG DIFFERENCE** whether **the creation (or destruction) of Shareowner Value is viewed from the perspective of *all* of a company's Shareowners *or* from the perspective of an *individual* Shareowner. *The difference can be seen in how Shareowners think and act, AND in how managers think and act!*"......

Sam looked at his watch........."Well, its almost 9:30, and you have a working day ahead of you tomorrow."

"Whoa Sam!" exclaimed Nancy, "You can't just stop here after that time bomb!"

"Right on!" said Tom.

"How can we continue?" asked Wendy.

"Well, I enjoy the conversation, and learning from you," said Sam. "And, I won't be offended if you don't want to continue! But for those who do, here is what I suggest. During the day everyone is scattered on the ranch. However, before breakfast, I usually have coffee on the porch. It's ready at 6:00. Also, after supper there is usually free time to sit and chat.....Your pleasure!"

"We'll see you for coffee!" said Tom. "Georgia and I usually have the eighteen wheeler rolling by 5:00, so 6:00 suits us fine! Just make sure the coffee is strong!"

John groaned at the thought of a 6 a.m. wakeup during vacation, but Debra said, "I'll be there!"

"I'll make plenty of coffee," grinned Sam. "It's a little thick though. We usually use spoons to drink it!......See you in the morning!"

With a little waive, Sam left the room.

Several members of the group continued with casual conversation about where they were from, what they did, and places they enjoyed in the West.

At 10 o'clock, Wendy and Nancy got up, collected Nancy's husband, Steve, and walked to their cabins. Nancy and Steve Patterson were from Boston where Steve was the Chief Financial Officer ('CFO') of a three billion dollar high tech firm. They were staying in cabin 11, 'The Pragmatist's Lair' with their preteen son and daughter, Fletcher and Emma.

Once Wendy arrived at her cabin, and slipped beneath the blankets, it didn't take her long to fall asleep!......Her last thought was that the week was off to a great start!

Measuring the Creation (or Destruction) of Shareowner Value!

Between two points in time (such as the purchase and sale of a stock), the creation (or destruction) of Shareowner Value is measured as follows:

Shareowner Value Creation (Destruction)	=	Cash Paid In Dividends (plus any earnings on that cash)	+	Increase (Decrease) in Market Value of Stock

7.

The Three Reasons that Stock Prices Change!

It was 5:15.

Wendy woke feeling refreshed. This time she knew why! Back East her time would have been 7:15; so in a manner of speaking, she had slept in!

She had a nice, warm shower, dressed in her jeans, cowgirl shirt and riding boots, and with Stetson in hand, headed for the coffee pot in the Dining Room. The air near the Lodge was filled with the delicious aromas of pancakes, syrup, bacon and sausage being served to the ranch hands. The hands ate an hour before the guests so that they could saddle the horses and begin other chores. The cooks and wranglers had already been up for at least two hours. The wranglers had rounded up the horses into the corral where the horses contentedly munched on grain.......The cooks brewed their magic.

Tom and Georgia were already at the coffee pot. Tom slowly poured Wendy a cup of rich, black coffee. She added more cream than usual, and the three of them walked to the south side of the porch. Wendy was glad she had worn her riding jacket because it was only 56 degrees, and with the light breeze, it seemed cooler. That would soon change.

As they walked onto the porch and looked out over the valley and pastures a thousand feet below, they watched the sun's bright yellow light flowing down the misting western mountains like rich butter melting down tall stacks of piping hotcakes.......

"Beat yuh!" teased Debra.

"Good morning!" welcomed Sam. "Grab a chair!"

With coffee cups steaming, Debra and Sam were already seated in the oversized, wooden, porch chairs, enjoying the early morning silence.

Small talk commenced, and the group quickly expanded adding Nancy and Steve, as well as Wendy's soon to be riding partners, Jim and Nancy Perrier.

The conversation promptly focused when Debra turned to Sam, and said, "Last night we agreed that Shareowner Value was created (or destroyed) based upon the change in stock price over time.......But, **what causes stock prices to change?**"

Sam paused, then replied. "Coming from one of the best business schools in the country, you must have some thoughts on that."

"I do!" said Debra, and then she paused tentatively.

"Share them with us!" encouraged Georgia.

"O.K.!......Here goes!" said Debra. "I believe that the basic value of a company is the *present value of its cash flow*.......This means that two things determine a company's stock price: (1) its cash flows (which include earnings) and (2) its cost of money. The cost of its money is used to calculate the current value (or present value) of *all* of the cash that the company will generate in the future."

Nancy interrupted with a clarifying question. "Debra, you said 'the present value of all the cash'. I assume that you mean both the cash received by the company as well as the cash paid out of it; in other words, **the *net* cash flow!** And by present value you meant **the *net* present value of all the cash flows?**"

"That's right!" said Debra, and she paused.

"Something must bother you about your definition, Debra, or you wouldn't have asked 'What cause stock prices to change?'" observed Sam.

"You're right, Sam, I do have a problem," mused Deborah. "**Stock prices fluctuate over time around** *the net present value of the cash flow* that I just mentioned.......But that's the problem; they fluctuate! I can't explain why!"

"I can explain that!" volunteered Jim Perrier, the broker from Atlanta. "Its called supply and demand! In my brokerage business there are many days when I see people willing to bid up the price of a stock just to own it, or conversely to quickly lower the price of a stock just to sell it."

"You mean that there are more buyers than sellers?" asked Debra's husband, John, who had just arrived on the porch.

"Not exactly!" laughed Jim. "I get a kick when I hear the financial press use that phrase.......The number of shares bought always equals the number of shares sold."

Jim continued. "The imbalance results when the people wanting to sell are more willing to lower the price just to get rid of the stock, than the people wanting to buy are willing to raise their offer price just to own the stock......or vice versa."

"I see what you mean," said John thoughtfully.

John took a sip of coffee while two squirrels provided comic relief as they chased each other around a tree trunk.

After a few minutes, Sam interrupted the entertainment, "Unless anyone has more comments on Debra's question, I'll summarize what the group has said.......It appears that *stock price is driven by three factors*: The first is the *cash flows* that a company generates; the second factor is the *cost of money* for the company, and the third factor is the current *'supply and demand'* for the company's stock."

"Sounds sensible to me!" said Steve, the CFO. "I've read studies showing that stock price movements are correlated only 18% with accounting measures such as EPS (earnings per share), but over 50% with cash flow measures. That's strong support for the group's conclusion!"

"Steve!" said Wendy. "You're saying that 50% of the change in a stock's price is due to a company's cash flow and its cost of money. The other 50% of the price change is due to supply & demand for the company's stock!?"

"That's correct!" said Steve.

"Awesome!" whispered Georgia. "50% versus 18%!".......The group could see her wheels turning!

The Three Factors that cause Stock Price to change:

1. *The Cash Flow of the Company*

2. *The Company's Cost of Money*

3. *Supply and Demand for the Company's Stock*

---

*Approximately 50% of a stock's price change
is due to a company's cash flow and its cost of money!....*

*.....The other half of the stock price change is due to
supply & demand for the company's stock.*

8.

Cash: The Least Common Denominator!

"Let's back up a minute!" said Jim Perrier. "When I talk with my brokerage customers, I talk about earnings, earnings per share (EPS), price to earnings (P/E) ratios and similar terms. What's this about cash flow and present value of cash flow?......Have I been looking at the wrong thing?"

"It's a little early in the morning, Jim, but since you raised the question, I'll try to explain it," responded Debra. "Its actually pretty simple!.........As you know, as a group, investors look at a wide range of investment alternatives before they invest. They want to get the best return for the risk they're taking!......They look at real estate, commodities, stocks, bonds, and international investments to name a few. Since all of these are accounted for differently, investors need a single, simple, yet comprehensive measure of value which can be used to compare all of the different investment alternatives on the same basis."

Debra took a sip of coffee, then continued, "In their search for a comprehensive measure of value, a number of knowledgeable investors have discovered that **cash is the least common denominator across all** investments. **With respect to companies**, since cash flow includes earnings as well as other sources and uses of cash, **cash flow is also a more inclusive measure than earnings."**

Debra paused, "Let me use bonds and stock in an example of how two alternative investments can be evaluated using cash flow."......

"My first problem in valuing bonds is that they don't have earnings; but stocks do! Therefore, traditional measures such as P/E (price to earnings) ratios don't work in valuing bonds. But, as I look further, **the key similarity between bonds and stocks is that they both have cash flow.** Let me show you how cash flow can be used to value these two different investments beginning with a bond."

Debra continued, "As I said, a bond is a contract by the bond issuer to pay a principal amount of, say, $1,000, at maturity, and a fixed dollar amount of interest of $100 at the end of each year. **I am going to assume that my bond is perpetual—meaning that it has no maturity date and pays the interest forever.** *You will see why in a minute.* As a final assumption, I will assume that current interest rates are 10%........Here, let me use this piece of paper to sketch the cash flows over the first ten years. The amount in each box is the cash flow which occurs at the end of that year."

BOND

	Total PV	Year 1	Year 2	Year 3	Year 4	Year 5	Year 6	Year 7	Year 8	Year 9	Year 10
Annual Cash Flow (Interest)		$100	$100	$100	$100	$100	$100	$100	$100	$100	$100
Terminal Value Cash Flow										?	

"Why did you write a question mark?" asked Georgia.

"Every year after year 10 we'll get an interest payment of $100. We need to put a value on that cash." said Debra.

"The way to value the cash after year 10 is to assume that at the end of year 10, someone is going to buy the bond from us. If the buyer wanted to earn 10% interest, then the value he would pay would be calculated by dividing the $100 annual interest by 10% ($100/10%); that equals $1,000. The proof of this is that if you invested $1,000 and received $100 per year, what interest rate have you earned? The answer is 10% ($100/$1,000)."…..

"So now," said Debra as she penciled in the $1,000, "we can put the $1000 that we sell the bond for at the end of year 10 into our cash flow diagram. **We call this the *Terminal Value* because it is the full value of the investment when we end or 'terminate' our investment by selling it at the end of year 10."**

BOND

	Total PV	Year 1	Year 2	Year 3	Year 4	Year 5	Year 6	Year 7	Year 8	Year 9	Year 10
Annual Cash Flow (Interest)		$100	$100	$100	$100	$100	$100	$100	$100	$100	$100
Terminal Value Cash Flow											$1,000

"That's pretty clear," said Nancy, "but, from my classes in engineering economics, I know that a dollar 10 years from now isn't the same as a dollar today!"

"Right!" said Debra. "So we 'discount' the future dollars to today's value—'the Present Value (PV)' at the 10% market interest rate. We apply a different discount factor to each year, and then add them. When we do that, we get the following numbers."……

"Debra, wait! Take one minute to explain the 'discount rate' and 'discount factor'!" said Tom.

"Certainly!" replied Debra. "We are assuming that any cash will earn a 10% per annum rate of return. Receiving $100 one year from now, is the same as receiving $91 today. The reason is that the $91 today invested at 10% will earn $9 interest by the end of year one. $91 + $9 = $100. Since the $91 is a 'discount' to the $100 and the rate used to calculate the discount is 10%, **we call the 10% the '*discount rate*.'"**

She continued, "The '*discount factor*' is a shortcut way of determining the amount of money you must start with in order to have the $100 at the end of a certain number of years. You can look the discount factor up in a table or calculate it using a calculator. In our one-year example above, we need to multiply the ending $100 by a discount factor of 0.91 to determine our starting cash of $91.......If we wanted to know how much we would have to start with in order to have $100 at the end of *two* years, assuming a 10% rate of return, we could also calculate the discount factor through trial and error as follows:

	Beginning Principal		Interest Rate		Beginning Principal		Ending Principal
Year 1	$ 83	x	10 %	+	$ 83	=	$ 91
Year 2	$ 91	x	10 %	+	$ 91	=	$ 100

"So, the two year discount factor for a 10% interest rate is 0.83 calculated as the first year beginning principal of $83 divided by the desired Year 2 ending principal of $100 ($83 / $100)." said Debra.

"Thanks, that makes sense and helps a lot!" said Tom.

Nancy then wrote the present values on the piece of paper. "I have worked this example a number of times and remember the numbers. While we don't usually show all of the discount factors, I will make an exception and write them for each year together with the present value of the cash flow for each year, so that you can see how they add up."

BOND

	Total PV	Year 1	Year 2	Year 3	Year 4	Year 5	Year 6	Year 7	Year 8	Year 9	Year 10
Annual Cash Flow (Interest)		$100	$100	$100	$100	$100	$100	$100	$100	$100	$100
Discount Factor*		0.91	0.83	0.75	0.68	0.62	0.56	0.51	0.47	0.42	0.39
PV of each year's Annual Cash Flow	**$614**	$91	$83	$75	$68	$62	$56	$51	$47	$42	$39
Terminal Value Cash Flow											$1,000
Discount Factor*											0.39
Present Value of Terminal Value Cash Flow	**$386**										$386
Net Present Value (NPV)	**$1,000**										

* For presentation convenience, all discount factors have been rounded to two decimal places.

Nancy pointed to the piece of paper and said, "Notice that the sum of the present values of all of the individual year's cash flows total $614 which is the Total Present Value of the Annual Cash Flow. As I mentioned, we normally don't show all of these discount factors and individual cash flows. In the future, I'll present the same information in shorthand as follows:"

BOND

	Total PV	Year 1	Year 2	Year 3	Year 4	Year 5	Year 6	Year 7	Year 8	Year 9	Year 10
Annual Cash Flow (Interest)	$614	$100	$100	$100	$100	$100	$100	$100	$100	$100	$100
Terminal Value Cash Flow	$386										$1,000
Net Present Value (NPV)	$1,000										

"Tom!" said Debra. "Notice the term *Net Present Value or 'NPV'* on the bottom line. This is the sum of the present value column. **We call it the *Net* Present Value because it is an algebraic sum—i.e. there are often positive and negative numbers in the column.** As you will see later, if a company has debt, it must be subtracted to determine the NPV or Enterprise Value of the company. We'll talk about Enterprise Value later.....**You can also think of the NPV as the total Cash Value of the bond or stock."**

"So," observed Nancy as she pointed to the piece of paper, "the Net Present Value of cash flow represents the 'arms length' price that an independent third party would pay for the stock or bond if they wanted to earn 10% p.a.!"

"Yes," said Jim, "but I still don't see **how this relates to a stock?"**

"Simple!" said Debra. "**A stock is nothing more than a set of Annual Cash Flows.** *The Annual Cash Flows consist of after tax operating earnings (often referred to as Net Operating Profit After Tax, or 'NOPAT'), plus non-cash items (such as depreciation and amortization) minus uses of cash (such as capital expenditures for equipment and working capital for receivables and inventory).* **Since a company has an infinite life, the Annual Cash Flows are perpetual—like the dividends in a perpetual bond.** Therefore, we need to include a Terminal Value that represents what someone would pay in Year 10 for the cash flows that occur after year 10. **If you owned a well managed company, *but which had no*** *growth,* and if it had $100 per year of Annual Cash Flow, the Annual Cash Flow and Terminal Value would look exactly like the bond which we just discussed, and can be shown as follows:"

STOCK

	Total PV	Year 1	Year 2	Year 3	Year 4	Year 5	Year 6	Year 7	Year 8	Year 9	Year 10
Annual Cash Flow	$614	$100	$100	$100	$100	$100	$100	$100	$100	$100	$100
Terminal Value Cash Flow	$386										$1,000
Net Present Value (NPV)	$1,000										

"But," said Wendy, "as you said, Debra, unlike a bond, a company may start out with cash *and* debt!"

Georgia interrupted. "Wouldn't a company's cash and debt be treated the same way that I treat cash and debt in my personal portfolio?....I would add cash and subtract debt to get the Cash Value of my portfolio....... We would do the same thing to get the Net Present Value (NPV)—or the total Cash Value—of the company."

"Exactly right!" replied Debra. "We can do this in our model by adding two lines to show cash and to subtract debt, just as Georgia suggested. We add the cash at the beginning of a time period as a *source* of cash flow, and the debt at the beginning as a *use* of cash flow. In this example, I will assume $300 of beginning cash (+) and $300 of beginning debt (-). For now, we will assume that they net, or cancel, each other out."

Debra then quickly added the cash and debt lines to the model for a stock on a second piece of paper:

STOCK

	Total PV	Year 1	Year 2	Year 3	Year 4	Year 5	Year 6	Year 7	Year 8	Year 9	Year 10
Annual Cash Flow	$614	$100	$100	$100	$100	$100	$100	$100	$100	$100	$100
Terminal Value Cash Flow	$386										$1,000
Cash	$300										
(Debt)	($300)										
Net Present Value (NPV)	$1,000										

"So," she observed, "*both a bond and a stock can be valued, and there-fore, compared, based upon the net present value of their cash flows.* If the cash flows, and the discount rate used are the same, the stock and bond will have the same value. In fact all investments can be valued based upon the present value of their cash flows."

"**But I still don't see why cash flows are better than earnings for valuing a company!**" said Jim.

"Jim, let's step back, and without being encumbered by the precedent of existing accounting practice, let's think about what we are really try-ing to do," said Sam.

"OK!?....." agreed Jim.

Sam continued,......"In the physical world we use different meas-ures for different purposes. For example, we use a yardstick to measure distance, a scale to measure weight, and a watch to measure time.......*In the financial world, we also need different measures!* ......Accounting is just one type of measuring device; it was created in a slower moving world to spread historic costs against revenue so that bankers could have a sense of whether they had adequate collateral for their loans.....As Debra is explaining, *we are trying to measure some-thing different! We are trying to measure value creation,* and we have defined value creation as the increase in the Net Present Value of the company's cash flow........Accounting, as currently structured, is not designed to measure the cash value of a company nor whether the company is increasing its cash value—the NPV of cash flow. *Since increasing the present value of cash is what creates value, we need a way to measure it!"*

Steve quickly injected his response to Jim's question. "Jim, let me add a different perspective to what Sam has said . ... As a Chief Financial Officer, who sees a wealth of financial data inside the company, I can assure you that earnings tell only a minor part of the story. The reason that earnings are deficient is that they are based upon arbitrary accounting rules which among other problems, (1) change over time, (2) are not applied the same by every company, (3) are different between countries, and (4) are not relevant to certain types of assets such as real estate. Let me give some examples.

- There are over 200 APB's, ARB's, FASB's[2] and other accounting pronouncements in the US, alone! Many change previous pronouncements.

- Even though the accounting profession has worked hard to set standards, *the standards allow management discretion in applying them* to different businesses and in different circumstances.......As a result between 1998 and 2000, the Securities and Exchange Commission (SEC) required over 464 public financial statements to be restated by US companies due to questionable management judgment in applying discretion to accounting standards.

- Companies headquartered in different countries report earnings using the GAAP (Generally Accepted Accounting Principles) accounting rules of that country. **As a result, two**

---

2. APB = Accounting Principles Board; ARB = Accounting Research Bulletins; FASB = Financial Accounting Standards Board

identical companies located in different countries will report different earnings simply because the accounting rules in the countries are different. Obviously, using the same P/E multiple on two different earnings numbers results in two different valuations for the identical companies. However, since cash flow is not distorted by the accounting rules, **the present value of cash flows for the two companies would result in identical values**.......*Like music and mathematics, cash flow is the same in any language!*

- Many types of real estate appreciate in value, yet accounting rules require them to be depreciated (expensed) on the income statement. The true value of real estate is the present value of the cash flows it will generate, *not* the accounting book value. Therefore, the value of some companies is under or over stated if the valuation is based upon P/Es or other accounting numbers.

- As we continue our discussions, I am sure that we will explore other major distortions that arise in valuing a company using P/E ratios rather than NPV of cash flow. For example, new accounting rules[3] no longer amortize goodwill related to acquisitions as an expense in the income statement. This increases earnings even though there is no change in cash flow, and therefore, no increase in Enterprise Value!"

As Steve caught his breath, Sam observed, "**There is another hidden advantage to using cash flow. It reinforces integrity in reporting!**.......**Cash flow has to 'reconcile' to 'cash in the bank.' Earnings don't!**....**Earnings just have to reconcile to other accounting numbers on the accounting statements!** Requiring management to explain cash flow reduces distortion caused by either changes in

---

3. FAS 142 *Goodwill and Other Intangible Assets*

accounting rules (including, the discretion which management has in applying the rules) *or* by rapid changes in technology and the business environment."

"You're right, Sam!" said Steve. "*Earnings* are an indicator of a company's results, but they are not as encompassing as cash flow, *and* they *do not consider the time value* (present value) *of money*. As we've said, Generally Accepted Accounting Principles ('GAAP') were designed to spread historical costs against revenue. They were never designed to measure creation of value; to do that, we need to measure changes in the net present value (NPV) of cash flows!"

Steve paused.

"If you don't mind Steve, I'd like to expand on something you said," observed Wendy.

"By all means!" Steve encouraged.

Wendy continued, "By focusing on the net present value of cash flow, you are forced to consider many years of the company's operations, *and*, as you said, the time value of money. When you use price to earnings ('P/E') ratios or similar accounting ratios, you are looking at *just one year's performance* which could materially deviate from normal operations."

"That's correct," said Steve, as he took a sip of coffee.

Georgia impatiently looked at Sam and said, "I think that there is a simpler way of saying all of this!"

"Have at it!" replied Sam with a smile.

"Earlier, we heard Steve say that 18% of a company's stock price is determined by EPS (earnings per share), and 50% by the present value of cash flow!"

"Go ahead!" encouraged Sam.

"Well!" concluded Georgia, "That means that cash flow is 2 ½ times more powerful than accounting earnings in determining share price!"

A stunned silence followed.....Sam let Georgia's observation sink in as he smiled and patted her arm.......He knew that this lady trucker knew how to make the rubber meet the road!

After reflecting on these comments for a few moments, Jim finally nodded thoughtfully and said, " I think I see!......Earnings are a 'fuzzy', one year, snapshot of a company, whereas the present value of cash flow is a clearer—although not perfect—motion picture which captures more angles of the present as well as looks into the future of the company and considers the time value of money."

"Well put!" said Steve.

Cash Flow: The Least Common Denominator!

Cash Flow is the "lowest common denominator" across all investments!

It takes into consideration all sources/uses of cash, and must reconcile with cash in the bank!

Earnings only have to reconcile to other accounting numbers, which are a function of management discretion in the application of arbitrary accounting rules.

The Net Present Value of Cash Flow is the most comprehensive measure of value across all investment alternatives!
It takes into consideration the time value of money.

Earnings are like a fuzzy snapshot of a company at a point in time.

Net Present Value (NPV) of cash flow is like a motion picture of a company; it captures more angles of the present and looks forward over time.

Cash flow is 2 ½ times more powerful than earnings per share in determining a company's share price!

9.

The Difference between Stocks and Bonds!

Jim continued, "We still have a few minutes before breakfast, and I need the answer to another key question.........Debra, you explained how a stock and a bond were alike. But, isn't there a difference?"

"There is a *MONUMENTAL* difference!" she replied.

"Please explain it!" requested Jim.

She finished a sip of coffee, nodded and continued, "Recall that a bond is a contract to pay principal and interest. All of the remaining cash flow generated by the company goes to the benefit of the Shareowners. **Therefore,** *the difference between a bond and a stock is the ability of the people in a company to grow the present value of cash flows!* **That is what belongs to the Shareowner.......And, it is this potential for growth in the net present value of cash flow which entices Shareowners to invest in a company.**"

Debra wrote new numbers on to a napkin. "**Let me show you how powerful the employees' work can be.** As I said, growing a company's Annual operating Cash Flows increases its present value, and therefore, its share price........Here's how it works in our example. Let's assume that the Annual Cash Flow grows 10% each year for ten years and then stops growing. Since the cash flow in year 10 is higher ($236 vs. $100), the Terminal Value is also higher by $1360 ($236/ 10% = $2,360 vs. $1,000). We assume that the discount rate remains constant at 10%."

STOCK OF A COMPANY GROWING @ 10% per annum.

	Total PV	Year 1	Year 2	Year 3	Year 4	Year 5	Year 6	Year 7	Year 8	Year 9	Year 10
Annual Cash Flow	$909	$100	$110	$121	$133	$146	$161	$177	$195	$214	$236
Terminal Value Cash Flow	$909										$2360
Cash	$300										
(Debt)	($300)										
Net Present Value (NPV)	$1,818										

"*Notice that the Net Present Value* of $1818 in this 10% growth case *is* $818 or *82% higher than the $1,000 in the no growth case*," concluded Debra.

Sam enthusiastically injected, "That's the power of properly directed, motivated employees!"

"Wow!" exclaimed Georgia. "Growing Annual Cash Flow *really* has a powerful impact on a stock's Cash Value (NPV)!"

There were many nods of agreement.

"Debra, you have covered a lot of ground this morning!" observed Wendy, "It's really helpful and sets the stage for one of my questions for tonight: '*Who* is responsible for creating Shareowner Value?'"

"That's a great place to start this evening," said Sam. Turning to Debra, he said, "Debra, I agree with Wendy! You have helped us shake the loop out of the rope this morning! Tonight we will learn how to use it. Great job!.......Now, let's feed some hungry hands!"

The Difference Between a Stock and a Bond!

The difference between a stock and a bond
is the ability of the people
in a company
to grow the net present value (NPV) of
the company's cash flow!

Growth in a company's cash flow
is the result
of
properly directed and motivated
employees!

10.

The Forgotten Shareowner!

At the designated time of 8:30 a.m., Wendy and her riding partners assembled at the barn. In addition to Wendy, this group included Jim and Patty Perrier with their three children—Paige, 7, Alexa, 8 and Jack, 10, Tom and Georgia Roman, and Ed and Susan Rogers from Charlotte. Debra and John Morgan changed riding groups because their two teenage daughters, Cassandra and Lauren, wanted to ride with some new friends.

Just as they completed introducing themselves, the guests turned to see two wranglers ride up at a full gallop. Dakota slid to a dismount and began directing other wranglers to bridle, cinch and lead horses to the guests. The other wrangler reined the handsome palomino gelding to a timely stop in front of them. The way the palomino and rider acted in unison, it was clear that this wrangler was an excellent horseman. The wrangler was wearing forest green, hunter style chaps with fringe and Ariel, ankle-height, English, riding boots. From underneath the 'Gus' cowboy hat, a cheery midwestern accent suddenly bid, "Good morning, wranglers! Welcome to the ST Bar! My name is Gina Evans, and I'll be your lead wrangler this week!"

Paige and Alexa were delighted to see a real, live cowgirl!

Gina scanned the guests as she spoke, "Besides your fun, our primary concern at the ST Bar is safety, especially around horses. While we get your horses ready, let me talk about horse safety before we go on a morning ride."

As Gina continued, Wendy was impressed that the ranch could attract smart, capable young people like Gina and Glen as wranglers for the summer. It made the guests feel comfortable.

Wendy's horse was a 15-hand buckskin quarter horse named 'Belle'. As she mounted, Wendy was glad that she had worn her old riding chaps. They gave her a sense of security in the saddle.

Gina led them out of the coral with Dakota riding drag. The first ride would include walking, trotting and two slow lopes—or canters as they were called back East. This mix let the guests get the feel of their horses, and let the wranglers observe the guests' riding abilities.

During the single file rides in the woods and up and down hills, the riding order began as family groups and gradually evolved into mini groups with common interests. The young people all rode together. Wendy followed Gina with Ed and Susan Rogers behind Wendy.

During the ride, they shared observations on the scenery and their background. Gina was a champion Event rider in the Midwest. When asked to describe Eventing, Gina often said, "Eventing is the 'triathlon' of horse competition and includes arena jumping and dressage competition as well as cross country." Gina had worked in the Treasury of a major company for five years, before returning to graduate school to work on her MBA. She had just finished the first year of her MBA at Wharton.......This was Ed and Susan's first ranch experience. They were celebrating their tenth anniversary. Ed was an equity analyst (a.k.a. 'stock picker') for a major investment bank. Susan worked for the Environmental Protection Agency.

As they rode, Wendy mentioned how much she was enjoying the unexpected conversations with Sam. Ed was intrigued, and asked Wendy to give him 'five' minutes of highlights as they rode.

Gina put the group into a trot, and then along an old logging trail, they broke into a rocking chair lope for a quarter mile. They ended on the edge of a long peaceful meadow, and walked to the shade of several Ponderosa Pine and Engelmann Spruce on the far side.

Gina dismounted, and dropped her lead line. "Let the horses take a 20 minute break."

She then helped others to dismount.

As the riders relaxed in the shade and sipped water from canteens, the horses grazed.

"Gina," said Wendy, "I am curious. With your financial background, do you ever talk finance with Sam?"

"Sure." replied Gina. "When we are opening the ranch for the guest season—and even occasionally during guest season—some of us sit around the Lodge fireplace after supper. As is natural, we talk about things of common interest. Some talk cattle, some talk about home and the future, and all of us talk about horses. But, occasionally, a small bunch of us, studying for our MBAs, will sit with Sam until midnight. We talk about financial concepts and how to make them work in the real world. We have fun challenging each other and trying to figure out how to cause people to create Shareowner Value."

"Sounds nice!" fancied Wendy..........."I notice that Sam insists on using the term Shareowner rather than stockholder, shareholder, stakeholder, or some other term."

"Yes,......if you listen to Sam, he almost speaks of the Shareowner with reverence." nodded Gina.

"Why is that?" asked Wendy.

"I think it's because Sam believes the best way to empower people to realize their personal potential is through free enterprise," said Gina. "He says that together, individual Shareowners and creative, hardworking employees have given us all a standard of living which is the envy of the world. He believes that an often forgotten key to that partnership is the willingness of some people, 'Shareowners', to forego consumption in order to let others use their money to earn a living,—and at the same time produce a return for the Shareowner."

Gina looked up and spoke with emphasis, "Sam says **that the term Shareowner better than any other term conveys the message that a *human being* owns a share of the company, and has made personal sacrifices in order to buy that share.**"

"One time we challenged Sam by saying that most shares were owned by institutions." Gina continued. "He looked us straight in the eye, and said, 'Just like company managers, those institutions are just intermediaries—fiduciaries—holding IRA, 401(k), profit sharing, retirement or other money for hard working people who are sacrificing or delaying spending so that the people in the company can benefit from using the money to make a living....In fact, part of the money that the institutions are investing probably belongs to the people in the company, so, the employees are investing in themselves.'"

Wendy interrupted, "It sounds like Sam believes that it's important for all of us to recognize that the Shareowner is a flesh and blood person, just like us, and that we owe them some loyalty for enabling us to earn a living using their cash."

"That's right!" said Gina. " I hope that you will continue your conversations with Sam. They're fun, and always bring out new ideas!"

"But," said Susan, "**haven't we seen enough of management and Boards taking action in the name of Shareowner Value which hurts the community?**"

"**Yes!**" Gina chewed on the sweet, tender end of a piece of grass she had plucked from the meadow. "**But, a lot of it occurs because managers are really managing to an accounting number, earnings per share (EPS), instead of managing in order to create Shareowner Value. These are two very different things!**......You should talk with Sam about this!"

"Thanks, Gina. I will." replied Susan.

"Mount up!" said Dakota.

"Can you check my stirrups?" asked Jack.

"Sure!" Dakota ambled over to Jack. "Do you know how to tell if your stirrups are the right length?"

"No." said Jack.

Dakota lowered his head so that his hat brim covered his smile. He spoke loud enough for everyone to hear. "Well,......if your knees hurt, the stirrups are too short.....If your butt hurts, the stirrups are too long.....If your knees and butt hurts, the stirrups are just right!"

Everyone laughed and continued their ride, enjoying the fresh, mountain air and the sunny day.

Who is this Forgotten Shareowner?

S/he is a Human Being!

The term Shareowner,

better than any other,

should remind us that a human being

owns a share of the company.

That human being

has made personal sacrifices

in order to let us use that money

to earn a living.

We have a responsibility

to return the money

to the Shareowner

together with a fair return!

Part II

Learning the Ropes.

11.

Who Creates Shareowner Value?

By supper, the guests were full of new ranch experiences!

Conversation was lively.......But, following a day in the saddle, the guests moved slow and gentle!......

After the meal, Sam walked over to a section of sofas and chairs in the Great Room arranged in a square with a heavy, pine 4' x 4' coffee table in the center. He was soon surrounded by a larger group of guests than on Sunday evening.

Observing the size of the group he asked, "What's going on here? You're reproducing!"

"It's the ideas that are breeding," laughed Nancy Patterson. "And all this good food forces us to relax after meals!"

"Yes, but the food is just replacing all the calories we're burning." said Georgia. "I never realized that horse back riding was so much exercise!"

Everyone nodded agreement........

"Speaking of exercise," said Debra, "my curiosity has been exercised since last night!"

"How so?" grinned Sam.

"Last night, you said that there was a BIG DIFFERENCE between how Shareowners and managers acted, depending on whether they

thought about the creation of Shareowner Value from the *perspective of all* Shareowners *or* from the perspective of the *individual Shareowner*.......What did you mean?"

Sam responded, "Well, Debra, my meaning will become clear if we first answer the question Wendy raised last evening, '*Who* **creates Shareowner Value?**'"

Nancy's analytical, engineering training reappeared. "Well, last evening we said that Shareowner Value is created (or destroyed) as measured by the increase (or decrease) in the Market Value of the stock. ......This morning we said that three things caused the stock price to move: (1) the company's cash flow, (2) the company's cost of money, and (3) supply and demand for the company's stock.....If we can identify who affects each of these three items, then we will know who creates or destroys Shareowner Value."

"That makes sense!" remarked Steve. "Let me start.....As CFO, I make sure that my management team understands that they control the company's resources, and that they need to manage those resources to increase the company's cash flow....So, as to *cash flow*, this *is management's responsibility!*"

At this point, Ed, the equity analyst from Charlotte, jumped in. "I second that! But, I also think that *cost of money is management's responsibility.* Aside from general changes in interest rates affecting everyone, management controls the amount of assets used in the business. That determines the total amount of money needed. Management then decides the mixture of debt and equity used to raise the money invested in the business and that is what determines the company's cost of money."

"I agree with Ed," said Wendy. "But, in a little bit, I would like to discuss how we calculate a company's cost of money—which I usually call 'cost of capital.'"

"Good idea!" Sam paused, waiting for other comments....."It appears that management controls, or is at least the dominant influence over cash flow and cost of money........Who wants to tackle the third factor: supply and demand for a company's stock?"

After a long pause, Jim, the stockbroker, said, "Yesterday, we defined creating or destroying Shareowner Value as the change in the Market Value of a stock over time. From my customer's viewpoint, the only two stock prices which ultimately matter are the price at which they buy the stock, and the price at which they sell the stock."

"Are those prices the same for all of your customers?" asked Sam

"No!" assured Jim. "They buy or sell at different times and at different prices."

"So, *who is responsible for selecting the buy and sell price for the individual stock?*" repeated Sam.

"*The individual Shareowner!*" replied Jim.

After another minute of silence, Debra exclaimed,......."Wow! ......This really gives me a different perspective on who creates Shareowner Value!......It changes the responsibility for actions affecting the value!"

"How so?" asked Ed.

Getting up, Debra walked over to a freestanding chalkboard behind one of the couches. The board was used to give guests their daily riding assignments. After asking Sam if it was OK to use the board, she flipped it over to the clean side, and spoke as she wrote.

"This is how I *USED* TO THINK ABOUT creation of Shareowner Value."

| Creation (Destruction) of Shareowner Value | Is = Caused By: | (Cash Flow | & | Cost of Money) |

ENTERPRISE VALUE
(Net Present Value of Cash Flow)

"Financial texts typically define creation (or destruction) of Shareowner Value as the change in the net present value (NPV) of cash flow of the company. This morning I used a simple model to show how to calculate the NPV of a company's cash flow. *The net present value of a company's cash flow is called the ENTERPRISE VALUE.* When you assume 'efficient markets', the current share price is supposed to equal the Enterprise Value.......Therefore, *in my old vision* Shareowner Value **and Enterprise Value were equal, and,** since management is the dominant determinant of Enterprise Value, then, *in my old vision*, ONLY **management actions determined share price, and therefore, creation (or destruction) of Shareowner Value was solely the result of management's actions.**"

"Based upon the new ideas we are discussing, *my new way of thinking* about Shareowner Value looks like this" Debra said this as she added the 'Supply & Demand' column and wrote down responsibilities.

	Management Responsibility	Shareowner Responsibility

$$\text{Creation (Destruction) of Shareowner Value} = \text{Is Caused By:} \left(\text{Cash Flow} \ \& \ \begin{array}{c} \text{Cost} \\ \text{of} \\ \text{Money} \end{array} \ \& \ \begin{array}{c} \text{Supply} \\ \& \\ \text{Demand} \\ \text{For a} \\ \text{Company's} \\ \text{Stock} \end{array} \right)$$

ENTERPRISE VALUE

(Net Present Value of Cash Flow)

"When you introduce short term supply and demand fluctuations as an additional determinate of share price, *the creation or destruction of Shareowner Value becomes DEPENDENT on the actions of* TWO parties: *management* who creates Enterprise Value *and the Shareowner* who makes the buy and sell decisions!"

"Interesting!......" said Sam. "Let's talk more about the implications."

"Wait, Sam!" said Wendy. "Don't managers have another responsibility?" asked Wendy.

"Proceed!" smiled Sam.

"Don't managers have a responsibility to *accurately* communicate current cash flow, and their best assessment of factors which will affect future cash flow?" asked Wendy.

"They can't fulfill their responsibility to Shareowners if they don't!" said Steve.

"I agree!" said Sam.

"Debra, you've led a great discussion!" exclaimed Steve. Then turning toward Sam, Steve said, "....Well, Sam, returning to your question on implications for creating Shareowner Value, Debra's conclusion means that Shareowners and equity analysts can't just point their finger at management when they don't make money on a stock. They need to ask themselves whether they made good decisions on the purchase or sale price of the stock."

"What constitutes a good decision on the purchase or selling price of a stock?" asked Sam.

"Whether a person is *buying below* the Enterprise Value or *selling above* the Enterprise Value," said Nancy. "*The Enterprise Value is the benchmark.*"

"*Why is the Enterprise Value the benchmark?*" asked Sam.

"Because!" replied Wendy. "*The stock price eventually regresses to the mean. The long term mean is the net present value of cash flows (NPV) which by definition is the Enterprise Value.*"

"Another implication," said Ed, "is that management should be rewarded based on whether they increase the Enterprise Value, not on increases (or decreases) in share price. Share price often temporarily deviates from Enterprise Value due to short-term supply and demand factors outside of management's control. Since management affects the cash flow and the cost of money for the company—the determinant of Enterprise Value—they should get paid for increasing Enterprise Value. Managers should not be rewarded (or hurt!) if the supply and demand in the stock market temporarily expands or contracts the price to earnings (P/E) multiple and nothing has changed in the underlying Enterprise Value."

Sam interjected, "In my judgment, Ed has just identified a pivotal issue in the practical process of creating Shareowner Value. I expect that we will discuss it later this week."

"What's that?" asked John.

"The basis for paying incentive compensation." replied Sam.

"There is another separate issue here for equity analysts!" said John. "Most investors do not have the time or knowledge to calculate

Enterprise Value. Equity analysts need to earn their pay by calculating the Enterprise Value of a company and stating their assumptions. That way the average Shareowner will have an additional benchmark in addition to the analyst's buy and sell recommendation."

Sam pointed to the board. "As Debra has shown, while efficient markets cause stock price to normalize (or regress) to the Enterprise Value over time, short term 'supply and demand' imbalances cause us to think differently about who has responsibility for the factors which create (or destroy) Shareowner Value. **Shareowners are responsible for decisions related to the purchase and sale of stock as well as decisions on who manages the company. Managers are responsible for creating (or destroying) Enterprise Value**—the net present value (NPV) of a company's cash flow."

Who creates (or destroys) Shareowner Value?

Management

*creates (or destroys) Shareowner Value
for all Shareowners
by their actions
which create (or destroy) Enterprise Value
(the net present value of cash flow).*

Shareowners

*create (or destroy) Shareowner Value
for themselves
by their decisions
on the price at which they buy and sell the stock.*

12.

Shareowners are Responsible for Buying and Selling at a 'Fair' Price!

"Wait!" said Tom. "Let's go over this again. **We said that the Shareowner is responsible for creating (or destroying) value for himself when he buys or sells the stock. I need some help! How do I know what is a 'fair' price for a stock?"**

Jim smiled. "Will Rogers, the cowboy philosopher from Oklahoma, had some advice on that. He said 'Don't gamble. Take all your savings and buy some good stock, and hold it till it goes up,…. then sell it……If it don't go up, don't buy it!'"

Sam laughed. "Well, I'm not sure that Tom wanted to hear 'Buy low; sell high!'…….. But, there is wisdom in Will's words, especially in light of what Wendy said earlier this evening. To paraphrase, recall that Wendy said that the Enterprise Value—the net present value of cash flow—is the 'mean' about which stock price fluctuates. We also agreed that Enterprise Value was the benchmark for a stock's value………I **suggest that Enterprise Value represents the *'fair' price* for a stock.**"

"Are you saying that the Enterprise Value is like a magnet that eventually pulls stock prices up if they are below it, and pulls stock prices down if they are above it?" asked Tom.

"Like water seeking its own level?" observed John.

"Exactly right!" said Debra. "In the end, a company—just like a bond—is not worth more or less than the net present value (NPV) of the cash flow in it! If an investor expects the same return as you (i.e. the same discount rate), then he will not pay more cash for the stock than the net present value of the company's cash flows."

"Explain that a little more." requested Tom.

"Sure!" said Debra. "Every asset that a company has can be converted to cash either by producing a product or service, or simply by selling the asset. But if the accounting book value of the asset is overstated, there is no magical potion—no 'Philosopher's Stone'- that can transform the asset's accounting book value into cash. Let me say it differently. **Just as there is no alchemy which turns lead into gold, there is nothing –including accounting wizardry—that can generate cash or cash value where there is none.**"

"So, let's expand on Tom's question, and discuss 'good' stock prices," said Georgia. "To me, a 'good' stock price is one that puts more cash in my pocket. So, if Enterprise Value is the 'fair' stock price, can I assume that a 'good' stock price happens if I buy a stock below its Enterprise Value and later sell the stock at a price above its Enterprise Value?"

"That's the heart of it!" replied Sam. "A Shareowner's definition of a 'good' price depends on whether he is buying or selling, but if he is disciplined, it is relative to the Enterprise Value. As we discussed, the 'Enterprise Value is the price of a stock which lets the Shareowner earn a 'fair return.' If you buy below that price and sell at or above that price, you get more than a fair return. So, in your lingo, **the Enterprise Value is a key benchmark for judging whether you got a 'good' price on the purchase or sale of a stock!**"

What is a 'fair' price for a Stock?

The equilibrium or 'fair' price of a stock
is the Enterprise Value –
the net present value of cash flow.
Enterprise Value is the price that gives the Shareowner a
'fair' return.

Buying below the Enterprise Value,

and selling above the Enterprise Value

increases the likelihood

that the Shareowner

will create Shareowner Value

for himself.

13.

Determining the 'Cost of Capital'!

"Sam, you've made it too simple!" said Wendy. "To compute the 'fair' price—or Enterprise Value—you need to have a discount rate! There are volumes of books written on calculating the discount rate!"

"Guilty!" replied Sam as he threw his hands to the sky as if being arrested.......
"But, there is a practical answer.......**Let's discuss the discount rate.....Earlier this evening, Wendy, I believe that you called it the 'cost of capital?' Can you describe the concept a little more?"**

"Sure." said Wendy. "To produce cash flow, a company needs to invest cash. *We call this investment cash 'capital'. The company gets its capital in the form of equity* from Shareowners *and debt* from lenders."

Wendy continued, "**Since both the Shareowners and the banks want a return on their investment, the investment capital has a cost to the company.** For example, the lenders want interest; Shareowners expect to earn a 'fair' return on their stock in the form of an increasing stock price and dividends. **When you calculate the weighted average of the returns earned by the lenders and Shareowners, the result is called the company's 'Weighted Average Cost of Capital' or 'WACC.'"**

Nancy's analytical mind had jumped ahead of the group as she said, "**Are you saying that *to break even, a company must generate enough*** *cash to pay interest on its debt and to cover a 'fair' equity return on the current Market Value of the stock to the Shareowner?"*

"**That's exactly what I am saying!**" replied Wendy. "Perhaps it will become clearer with an example."

"Yes!" said Jim. "Please give us a simple example of how the WACC is calculated."

"Certainly!" Wendy walked to the chalkboard and erased Monday's riding assignments. "Let's use an example from our personal lives. Just like a company, we all have a source of 'capital' in order to purchase a home, car or other things. Most of us have a mortgage and perhaps credit card debt.....If someone asked us 'What interest do you pay?' we could tell them 7% on the mortgage and 16% on the credit card. But, if they were to ask us for the total cash we had borrowed and the weighted average borrowing cost, we would need to do a calculation like this."

Wendy wrote on the board:

Source	Amount		Rate		Interest Amount
Mortgage	$ 100,000	x	7%	=	$7,000
Credit Card	50,000	x	16%	=	8,000
Total	$150,000				$15,000

"So, your weighted average borrowing cost is $15,000 of interest divided by $150,000 of principal, or 10%:"

$$\frac{\$15,000}{\$150,000} = 10\%$$

"Now, Wendy, show us the way you compute it for a company." said John.

"All we need to do is change the names and rates!" said Wendy as she made some changes to the chalkboard.

"Let's use 10% for the cost of Shareowner's equity," suggested Sam.

Source	Amount		Rate		'Cost'
Shareowner's Equity	$ 100,000	x	10%	=	$10,000
Interest Bearing Debt	50,000	x	4.2%	=	2,100
Total Capital	$150,000				$12,100

Wendy commented as she wrote, "As I said, the $150,000 represents the sum of the equity and interest bearing debt. Together they are called 'Capital'. We can calculate the company's 'Weighted Average Cost of Capital' or 'WAAC'. It is computed by dividing the total dollar 'Cost' of $12,100 by the "Total Capital' of $150,000."

$$\frac{\$12,100}{\$150,000} = 8.1\%$$

Debra frowned and said facetiously, "You are beginning to make things sound 'Sam simple'!"

Everyone laughed.

"Guilty!" said Wendy as she imitated Sam with her hands reaching for the sky.

There was more laughter from the group.

Debra continued, "Wendy, please explain to everyone the dollar amounts you used for Debt and Shareowner's Equity and the rates that you used!"

Wendy responded with a smile as she explained, "The amount of Shareowner's Equity is the Market Value of the company's equity at a point in time; it is the number of outstanding shares times the share price. It has nothing to do with the equity on the company's financial statements! Shareowners expect management to give them a 'fair' AFTER TAX return on the CURRENT Market Value of their equity investment, NOT the historic value of equity on the balance sheet.

"Why's that?" asked John.

"Let's use an example," said Wendy. " Assume that the Shareowner's equity on the company's balance sheet is $500, and that the Market Value of the Shareowner equity is $1,000. Further assume that Shareowner's need to earn 10% on their investment or they can go buy an S&P 500 stock index yielding 10% p.a. If you're the Shareowner, how much does management need to earn on the equity?"

Georgia immediately replied "$100!"

"Why?" asked Wendy.

"I need to earn 10% or $100 on the Market Value of my $1,000 investment, or I will sell my stock and buy the S&P 500 stock index to earn 10%." said Georgia.

"Suppose management was only earning $50 or 10% on the $500 'book value' of Shareowner equity?" asked Wendy.

Georgia thought for a moment, and then said, "I'm in trouble!"

"How so?" queried Wendy.

"Because if the buyer of my stock wants to earn 10%, and management is only earning $50, then the buyer will only pay $500 for my stock. I'll loose $500 of Market Value on my stock!" Georgia responded.

"Absolutely right!" said Wendy.

The group was silent as Wendy took a sip of coffee, then she turned to a discussion of debt capital. "The debt is the interest bearing debt on the company's balance sheet. The interest rate on the company's debt is the after tax cost of the debt. We use the after tax cost of debt, because the company gets a tax deduction for the interest. Therefore, the cash 'out the door' related to the debt is the sum of the interest paid to the lenders minus the reduced cash paid as taxes to the government, which results from the interest deduction on the tax return. In the example, I assumed that the company paid the lenders interest of 7%. Since the company's tax rate was 40%, the company received a tax deduction of 40¢ for each $1 of interest. (In other words, for every $1 of cash paid to lenders, the government let the company pay $0.40 less in cash to the government because of the $1 of interest deducted on the company's tax return.) As a result, the after tax cash cost of debt was only 4.2%, calculated as: 7% x (100%–40%)."

Then, with a knowingly, teasing smile, Wendy turned to Sam and said, "It is only fair that Sam addresses the equity rate of return, because that was my question to begin with."

Sam had a big grin on his face.

Nancy interrupted, "Before Sam discusses the equity rate of return, let me make sure that I understand.......Do I understand from your first example that management needs to earn $12,100 in after tax operating profit just to earn enough dollars to break even in paying the lenders their 4.2% and produce a 10% return for Shareowners?"

"That's correct! " said Wendy. "Conceptually, $2,100 (plus the $1,400 cash from lower income taxes) goes to the lenders. (i.e. The lenders get interest totaling of $3,500 in cash or 7% on their $50,000 loan.) The remaining $10,000 is the 10% after tax return on the $100,000 Market Value of equity."

"So, if a company only earns it's cost of capital, i.e. breaks even, it merely maintains the current Enterprise Value, and therefore, the share price stays where it is!?!" exclaimed Nancy.

"Right on!!!" enthused Wendy...."Just as in Georgia's example!"

Nancy continued, "So the WACC (Weighted Average Cost of Capital) gives Shareowners a measure in absolute dollars as well as in percent to judge whether management is generating enough cash flow to keep the stock price where it is. That also means, that to increase the stock price, management needs to earn a return on new investments which is greater than the WACC, and therefore, for the company as a whole, the dollars of NPV needs to increase each year if the stock price is to increase."

"Absolutely right!" said Wendy.

Two useful ways to think of the Weighted Average Cost of Capital ('WACC'):

1.
WACC is the after tax rate of return that a company must earn in order to pay:

interest on debt to its creditors

and

a 'fair' return to its Shareowners on the Market Value of their investment!

2.
WACC gives Shareowners a benchmark in absolute dollars and in percent to judge whether management is generating enough cash flow to keep the stock price where it is.

To increase Share Price,
Management must earn more than WACC on its investments!

14.

What is a 'Fair Return' to Shareowners?

"OK, Sam, we need your help! You put us in a 'Catch 22'!" Ed Rogers admonished lightly.

"Yeah!" taunted Debra, Susan and Jim in unison.

Ed continued, "We have defined the Enterprise Value as the 'fair' stock price. But, to calculate the Enterprise Value, we need to know the 'fair return' that Shareowners should expect in order to blend it with the cost of debt to calculate the WACC (Weighted Average Cost of Capital) used as the discount rate."

Sam raised his arms into the air again and chuckled. "OK!….OK!….. Uncle!"

He put down his coffee cup, slowly leaned forward with his elbows on his knees and began.

"When you are out on the range and a problem comes up, whether it is caused by the weather, your horse or your own human nature, you learn to make do…..*You find a practical solution*!"

He looked up at the group. "Debra, Wendy and Steve can tell you about books and theories which have been written on calculating

Enterprise Value and 'fair return' to Shareowners. Most of them contain a lot of good thinking. However, *one problem* is that they are so refined that most people don't understand them or can't get the data to do the calculations. *A second problem* is that the theories assume continuous markets. They don't anticipate *sudden* adverse events that can dramatically affect a stock's price in minutes, let alone weeks. Examples include litigation scares (e.g. asbestos litigation impacting stock prices of Dow, USG, Halliburton, etc.) credit downgrades or misleading financial statements (e.g. Enron, etc.)"

He sat straight, hands in motion. "So for what it is worth, here is my horse sense on the subject."

"Just like Georgia, **my goal in investing is to increase the cash in my pocket—to increase my purchasing power. To do that, I need to earn more than inflation. I also want to be rewarded for the risk that I am taking.**"

"Over the past 70 plus years, the S&P 500 stock index has earned about 8% above inflation. That's a compound rate and includes dividends."

"The S&P 500 provides a good diversified benchmark for an equity investor. **An equity investor should earn at least the return on the S&P 500 otherwise he has an** *opportunity cost* (or loss) equal to the difference between the S&P 500 return and the return on the stock(s) he buys........Therefore, it seems to me that if I earn 8% above inflation on a stock, I have earned a fair return on the risk, and I have increased my purchasing power—cash in my pocket."

"Now, obviously, I won't bet my whole grub stake on just one stock. I would own a diversified portfolio of stocks."

"There are those who will tell you that you should earn more or less on a particular stock because of its riskiness. They use the term Beta, and say that they can calculate it. A Beta of 1.0 represents a return equal to the S&P 500. If a stock's Beta is above 1.0—say it's 1.2—it is 20% more volatile—'risky'—than the S&P 500........Well, in a day and age when 'blue chip' stocks with Betas below 1.0 (i.e. 'low risk') can go to junk bond status in the space of six months;......and when companies too young to have a Beta (*OR earnings*) can go to multiples of 50 times SALES, *I'm not so sure of the practicality of Beta for the average investor— or management.*"

"Refining Betas is a legitimate academic pursuit. But when major investment firms, brokers and investment bankers practice portfolio pumping (i.e. when money managers buy additional stock in companies that they already own in order to drive up their price on the last day of the month or quarter in order for the money manager to increase their performance fees) and similar practices, it is difficult to believe that refinements in Beta calculated using that data are of practical value."

"**If I can earn inflation plus 8% on a diversified portfolio, I figure that I am doing as well as this simple cowboy can do to get a 'fair return'.**"

"But, I want to make a common sense point here! **I *never* expect to earn less than inflation plus 8% on any individual stock** when I buy it."

"I have heard some argue that if Beta is low risk (i.e. less than 1) I should be willing to earn say 5% above inflation on a stock."

"Nonsense!"

"**When** utilities (which are low risk based upon historic Beta calculations) get legislated into bankruptcy in two years by price caps (California);......**When** airline stocks fall 50% in three days due to tragic global events (September 11, 2001);......**When** a $175+ billion company's stock falls 99% and goes bankrupt in slightly over a year— destroying $90 billion of Market Value—due to exceptionally bad judgment by the Board in allowing officers to do business with the company for their own account (Enron);......**Does it make sense to take any equity position without expecting to earn a return at least equal to the S&P 500?.....** *No matter* **how theory attempts to quantify it, common sense says that you're taking equity risk! Common sense dictates that** when you take equity risk, you should get a minimum return equal to the market's return!"

Sam sat back in the chair and changed direction.

"Instead of a return above inflation, some will argue that you should earn a return above a 'risk free' rate of return such as 10 year treasuries. That's nice theory, and creates short term trading rationales for arbitrageurs. But, there is a major defect in this thinking: Companies manage in the real economy, not the financial markets. When the Fed (Federal Reserve Board) manages interest rates up or down 2% in 6 months, it is not reasonable to expect that companies can adjust the return on their portfolio of long-term business investments in such a short time frame. If interest rates go up two percent, but inflation is flat, companies can't increase prices to get a higher return. Their cash flows—which create Shareowner Value—are more correlated with what happens in the real economy than with what happens in the financial markets. .....As a result, company managers need a reasonably stable medium term target rate of return related to the real economy in order to make corporate investment decisions.......This difference between the short term financial market perspective of traders and the pragmatic fact that managers need to invest longer term in the real economy will always create trading opportunities when market interest rates change. This is part of the supply and demand element of stock prices."

"So, let me conclude."

"Practically speaking, a 'fair return' for Shareowners is the long term real return of the S&P 500 stock index plus inflation. That *real return* is reasonably stable over the years at about 8%. For practical purposes, I add that 8% real return to a projection of inflation over the next year in order to calculate the rate of return to expect on stocks for the foreseeable future. I think that it is more appropriate to look ahead than backward. For example, if inflation is projected to be 2%, then I use 2% plus 8% or 10% as my expected return on equities."

The group was silent........Pensive!

Steve spoke up. "Sam, as a corporate financial officer, I have to wrestle with these issues in one form or another almost daily. The conclusion you have reached in my opinion is pragmatic. It is something a corporate manager can work with."

"Someday I would like to learn more about your comment on real rates of return and arbitrageurs, but from an M&A point of view with respect to long term Shareowners, I can live with your conclusion." said Wendy.

"Obviously, your conclusion embraces basic financial theory, but treads heavily on more refined aspects of those theories." said Debra. "But, I'd like to hear more about the practical applications of your conclusion. I want to understand the applications and their implications, so that I can go back and think about the theory later."

"Sam, I'm ready to call it a night." said Ed, "But, tomorrow, I'd like to talk about how investors and managers should use WACC (Weighted Average Cost of Capital)."

"That's a good place to start in the morning." said Sam. "My thanks for your patience and insights this evening. Have a good night's rest! You will need it for the cattle tomorrow!"

After returning to his cabin, Steve lay awake enjoying the baying of the coyotes;......anticipating tomorrow's events.

What is a 'fair return' to Shareowners?

*A 'fair return' to Shareowners
is the long term real return of the S&P 500 stock index
plus inflation.*

*That 'fair return' is currently the Consumers Price Index (CPI) plus an 8% real
return.*

15.

Shorthand for Determining if Management is Creating Enterprise Value!

It was 5:40 a.m. when Steve showed up on the porch, and sat down.

Sam was already in a chair writing notes in a little, black, calendar book.

"I see that you are still making those 'to do' lists like you used to." observed Steve.

"Can't break the bad habit!" grinned Sam. Then with genuine warmth he said, "Glad you and Nancy could make it this week! I hope that the kids have a great time on the ranch!....I expect that you will make your own entertainment during these sit downs with Ed and Debra."

"Well," replied Steve, "sharing interesting ideas is always fun! And as you know, there are only a few of us who bring the perspective of trail worn corporate finance officers. Perhaps our comments will be useful to others."

"Besides," Steve added, "I'll learn something!"

Sam smiled and nodded.

They sat sipping coffee and basked in private morning thoughts while Sam continued adding to his list.

During the ten minutes after 6 a.m., Ed, Debra, Wendy, Georgia, Tom and other 'regulars' drifted to the porch with hot chocolate or coffee.

Three new people also sat down: Jose Mendoza who 25 years ago founded and owns a $400 million manufacturing company located in Michigan, and Barb and Mitch Thompson. Barb is the CEO of a $5 billion consumer products company listed on the NASDAQ. Barb's husband, Mitch, is Senior Vice President of Human Resources for another major consumer products company.

Ed began the group conversation. "If its OK with everyone, I'd like to continue where we left off yesterday?"

Members of the group nodded agreement.

Ed continued. "Last evening, we said that Shareowner Value is created (1) when Shareowners make the right purchase and sale decisions on a stock relative to its Enterprise Value, and (2) when Management increases Enterprise Value. We defined Enterprise Value as the net present value of a company's cash flow using WACC (Weighted Average Cost of Capital) as the discount rate."

Ed continued, "These ideas have some powerful implications, but I'm not sure that I see them all. Can we explore how Shareowners know if managers are creating Enterprise Value?"

"Steve, you have worked with these ideas. How about kicking off the topic?" asked Sam.

"Glad to." replied Steve. "Let's start by repeating what we have agreed. We agreed that managers have one primary responsibility: To increase Enterprise Value—net present value (NPV) of the company's cash flow.......From experience, I can assure you that there is no alchemy to it, just discipline and hard work!"

'"Two ideas have been helpful to me in developing a shorthand which I use with my management team to judge if managers are creating

Enterprise Value. The ideas have their roots in Nancy's observations last evening..........She observed that WACC ('Weighted Average Cost of Capital') provides a benchmark in dollars and in percent to determine if management is earning enough to break even—i.e. to keep the Enterprise Value where it is.

Steve then broke his thought, "Let me illustrate my idea beginning with a question.......If you borrow $100,000 for 1 year at 10%, and invest it at 11%, how much value have you created for yourself?"

Patty Perrier responded, "1% on $100,000."

"Right!" said Steve. "Why didn't you say 11%?"

"Because 10% had to be paid to the banks. 11% minus 10% equals 1%," said Patty.

"Good!" agreed Steve. "Creating (or destroying) value in percent terms, only occurs if you earn a higher (or lower) percentage rate of return than the cost of the money you are investing."......

"For example, you would be destroying value if you borrowed money at 10% and invested it at 8%. The destruction rate is 2%."

Steve looked at Patty. "If you had borrowed the money for 10 years instead of just 1 year, what would your answer have been?"

"The same, 2% for each year-2% per annum," she replied.

Steve reached for a pen and paper. As he wrote, he spoke, "Let me write what Patty just said. Using percent gives you a rule of thumb for the value created or destroyed over the life of a project or acquisition.......For example, if the project had a cash flow rate of return of 11%—often called the Internal Rate of Return (IRR[4])—and the WACC was 10%, then creation of value is shown in the first example."

---

4. The Internal Rate of Return (IRR) is the after tax rate of return which equates the cash invested in a project with the after tax cash flows generated by the project over its life.

	Annual % Created or (Destroyed)	=	Annual % Return on the Investment	-	Annual % Cost of Cash Invested
Annual % Creation:	1%	=	11%	-	10%
Annual % (Destruction):	(2%)	=	8%	-	10%

"On the other hand, the second example shows what happens if management invests in a project forecast to earn 8%, while the company's WACC is 10%. In this case, the investment will *destroy value at a rate of 2% p.a. over the investment's entire life.* As we will probably discuss later, **this is critical in the context of investing in *acquisitions* as well as ordinary business assets.**"

"To repeat," said Steve, "if we have a constant return and a constant cost of money in percent terms, we can use it as a shorthand to think of the value created or destroyed *over the life of the project or over a series of years.*"

Steve continued, "There is a second way that we can look at our example. Let me ask the question again,.........'If you borrow $100,000 for 1 year at 10%, and invest it at 11%, how much value have you created for yourself?"

"I can answer it in terms of cash in my pocket!" said Georgia emphatically.

"Go ahead!" encouraged Steve.

"I have put $1,000 of cash in my pocket! At 11%, I earn $11,000, but I have to pay $10,000 to the bank," replied Georgia.

"That's right," said Steve." What happens if you only earn 9%?"

"I have lost (or destroyed) $1,000 of cash," she responded. "I have income of $9,000, but expense of $10,000."

"Let me write what Georgia just said," said Steve.

$ Value Created or (Destroyed)	=	$ of Income	-	$ Cost of money invested to make the Income

or

$ Value Created or (Destroyed)	=	$ of Income	-	($ Invested x Cost of $ Invested)

"For example:"

$ Creation:	$1,000	=	$11,000	-	($100,000 x 10%)
($ Destruction):	($1,000)	=	$9,000	-	($100,000 x 10%)

"When the formula is expressed in dollars, it is often called the formula for Economic Profit ('EP') or Economic Value Added ('EVA'[5])....It shows *the dollars of Economic Profit* which you have *created or destroyed* for yourself *over a period of time such as a year*."

Steve concluded, "**Economic Profit expressed in dollar ($) terms and percent (%) terms are two extremely simple, yet powerful ideas. When applied to a company, they form a *shorthand* which can be used (1) as a basis for communicating, empowering and motivating every person in the company to create Enterprise Value, and (2) as a rule of thumb for determining if Enterprise Value is being created in any given time period.** These concepts also affirm the fact that the principles of making money in a company are no different or more complex than the principles that a person applies to making money in their personal affairs."

"This is fascinating," said Barb.

"How so?" asked Sam.

---

5. EVA® is a registered trademark of Stern Stewart & Co.

Barb responded. "Until I listened to the conversations yesterday and today, it never occurred to me that equity capital had a 'cost' just like debt. And I certainly didn't know that I had to earn a cash return of inflation plus 8% on it just to 'breakeven' and to keep the stock price where it is!".......

She paused, then continued, "**This simple idea of Economic Profit brings home to me, that in spite of the sophisticated corporate finance that I studied in graduate school,** *the only way a company increases its value is to earn more than its cost of money—just like I have to do with my personal investments!*"

Barb shook her head in amazement, "This is very straight forward, but somehow lost in the pursuit of accounting EPS (earnings per share)!.........Later this week, I would like to understand how to apply these ideas to incentive plans."

"That would be very worthwhile!" seconded Mitch.

"We'll do it!" said Sam.

Shorthand to Determine if Management is Creating Enterprise Value:

To create Enterprise Value, Management must earn more than the cost of the capital used to create it!

This means:

1. In a given time period

—for example, a year—
The dollars of income must be greater than the dollar cost of the capital used to create the income. The formula is:

$ Value Created or (Destroyed)	= $ of Income	-	($ Invested x Cost of $ Invested)

Also expressed as:

Economic Profit (or 'EP')	=	Net Operating Profit after Tax (NOPAT)*	-	(Capital x WACC)

* plus non cash items such as Goodwill amortization.

OR

2. Over the project life:
the percent return (IRR) on the project must exceed the WACC!

This applies to all investments, including acquisitions!

Annual % Created or (Destroyed)	=	Annual % Return on the Investment	-	Annual % Cost of Capital Invested

16.

What Actions Create Enterprise Value?

Ed directed a question to Steve. "Steve, you have obviously thought a lot about creating Enterprise Value. Perhaps you can help me.......Often a company will issue a press release about future actions, or when I visit with management in my capacity as an equity analyst, management will make statements about what they are doing to increase sales, or margins or earnings. **Is there some quick shorthand that I can use to estimate the impact of management actions on Enterprise Value?** It would really be helpful if I had a quick estimate of the impact, so that I could immediately challenge management with a follow up question such as, 'But that action will only increase Enterprise Value by 'x' amount! Is that all you can do?'......Can you give me some insights into what I should be looking for in order to estimate the impact of actions on the share price?"

Georgia corrected Ed, "You mean the impact of management's actions on Enterprise Value, *NOT* share price!"

"Err....right!" said Ed. "Management controls Enterprise Value, *not* share price (Market Value)."

There were more than a few smiles in the group.

"I would be glad to give you some rules of thumb," replied Steve. "You are asking me about tools that I developed to help me manage!......Everyday my operating managers come into my office with new ideas, and it's my job to help them understand how to structure the ideas to create Enterprise Value. To be effective, I don't have time to run detailed numbers on each idea. So, I took one of Sam's simple models, in fact very similar to what Debra showed us yesterday morning, and did some sensitivity analyses to develop rules of thumb."

Steve reached into his pocket, "In fact, believe it or not, I saved the two pieces of paper which Debra wrote on yesterday morning. I thought that they might be useful later. Let me just add a sales line and a percent operating margin line to each of them, so that I can show you how I get my rules of thumb."

Steve wrote and then put the two pages on the porch coffee table for all to see. He showed them the Enterprise calculation for a no growth company and for a company growing 10% p.a. for 10 years.

Enterprise Value of a NO GROWTH Company

	Total PV	Year 1	Year 2	Year 3	Year 4	Year 5	Year 6	Year 7	Year 8	Year 9	Year 10
Sales		$1,000	$1,000	$1,000	$1,000	$1,000	$1,000	$1,000	$1,000	$1,000	$1,000
Annual Cash Flow	$614	$100	$100	$100	$100	$100	$100	$100	$100	$100	$100
% Margin		10%	10%	10%	10%	10%	10%	10%	10%	10%	10%
Terminal Value Cash Flow	$386										$1,000
Cash	$300										
(Debt)	($300)										
Enterprise Value (Net Present Value)	$1,000										

Enterprise Value of a Company GROWING @ 10% per annum.

	Total PV	Year 1	Year 2	Year 3	Year 4	Year 5	Year 6	Year 7	Year 8	Year 9	Year 10
Sales		$1,000	$1,100	$1,210	$1,330	$1,460	$1,610	$1,770	$1,950	$2,140	$2,360
Annual Cash Flow	$909	$100	$110	$121	$133	$146	$161	$177	$195	$214	$236
% Margin		10%	10%	10%	10%	10%	10%	10%	10%	10%	10%
Terminal Value Cash Flow	$909										$2,360
Cash	$300										
(Debt)	($300)										
Enterprise Value (Net Present Value)	$1,818										

"Before we talk about the rules of thumb, we need to identify what factors actually drive Enterprise Value. I call these factors the '*Value Drivers*'. There are *only five of them*! They are common to all companies and are what management must act on to create Enterprise Value."

"How did you identify the Value Drivers?" asked Barb.

Steve responded, "Since Enterprise Value is the net present value (NPV) of a company's cash flow, I looked at each line in the model and asked how do changes in this line affect the NPV of cash in a company."

Steve added, "In this discussion, let's let Annual Cash Flow represent the company's Net Operating Profit After Tax ("NOPAT") as well as changes in capital (both working capital and net capital investment) necessary to support the change in NOPAT. *More detailed models would show the changes in capital as separate line items.*"

Steve continued, "While there are many illusions of value creation, when you study the two examples and look at how changes in each line affect the NPV (or Enterprise Value) you conclude that *there are only five 'Value Drivers' which create Enterprise Value!* They are:

1. *Increase sales growth.* However, it must be internal organic growth, *NOT* sales acquired through acquisitions;

2. *Increase the Margin of Net Operating Profit after Tax ('NOPAT');*

3. *Reduce assets (capital) required to produce a given NOPAT.* This immediately increases cash in the bank or reduces debt;

4. *Make acquisitions that have a return higher than WACC (Weighted Average Cost of Capital).* The cash return above WACC when discounted to the present represents the total increase in the Acquirer's NPV (or Enterprise Value) resulting from the acquisition;

5. *Reduce the WACC through changes in the mix of debt and equity.* Up to a point, increasing debt usually decreases the

WACC. Using a lower WACC to discount the cash flows results in a higher NPV or Enterprise Value."

Steve commented further, "These are the only actions which increase Enterprise Value. But, let me elaborate a little further on how each of the actions increases the NPV of cash flow:

- **Increasing sales** can be accomplished either by increasing price or unit volume as well as through sales of 'newly invented' products/services. The sales must be profitable, including covering the cost of the incremental capital required to support them;

- **Increasing the NOPAT margin** on existing sales can be done through cost reduction or changing product mix;

- **Reducing the assets** (e.g. receivables, inventory, plant or equipment) required to produce a given amount of operating profit frees up cash by letting the company get cash for assets *no longer used*;

- **Acquiring cash flow in the form of acquisitions** increases net present value of cash flow *ONLY IF* the rate of return on the acquisition exceeds the WACC. *I want to talk about acquisitions later. Aside from poor management of the business, acquisitions are the largest destroyer of Enterprise Value!*

- **Decreasing the discount rate, i.e. WACC,** can be accomplished through share repurchases or by increasing debt (up to a point) in the company's capital structure. Share repurchases done at a price below the Enterprise Value per share decrease WACC. Conversely, issuing shares typically increases WACC. Action affecting the other four Value Drivers usually affects the amount of capital used in the business, and therefore, the WACC."

Sam said, "Steve, that's an excellent summary of the factors which managers can use to change Enterprise Value!"

"Steve!" exclaimed Wendy. "I just noticed that **you can arrive at the same conclusions by studying the Economic Profit (EP) formula.**"

Wendy spoke as she scribbled the Economic Profit formula on a napkin and pointed to the different variables. "If you ask yourself, what 'creates' Economic Profit, you see that the same five 'Value Drivers' that Steve listed on his napkin increase the EP. For example:

- Increasing sales increases NOPAT;

- Increasing margins increases NOPAT;

- Decreasing assets reduces capital;

- Decreasing WACC increases EP by reducing the $ cost of capital; and

- Also, if the cash NOPAT of the acquisition is greater than the cost of the acquisition x WACC, then the acquisition will create Economic Profit for the acquirer's Shareowners over its life!"

$$
\begin{array}{l}
\text{Economic} \\
\text{Profit (or 'EP')}
\end{array}
=
\begin{array}{c}
\text{Net} \\
\text{Operating} \\
\text{Profit after} \\
\text{Tax} \\
\text{(NOPAT)}
\end{array}
- (\text{Capital} \times \text{WACC})
$$

"That's excellent insight, Wendy!" said Steve. "It shows how the Economic Profit formula can be an additional 'shorthand' tool to understand whether certain actions will increase or decrease Enterprise Value.......But, I still haven't satisfied Ed by giving him rules of thumb for estimating the size of the impact of certain actions on Enterprise Value."

With a frown on his face, Ed nodded agreement.

Management must impact one or more of these five Value Drivers if Enterprise Value is to be created:

1. *Increase Sales (through increases in price or unit volume at a positive Economic Profit).*

2. *Increase the NOPAT margin.*

3. *Reduce Assets used in the Business (The reduction must be real, NOT just 'balance sheet dressing'!).*

4. *Acquire Sales, (But, only if the rate of the return on the acquisition exceeds the acquirer's WACC!).*

5. *Decrease the Weighted Average Cost of Capital (Consistent with Business Risk!).*

17.

The Impact of Management Actions on Enterprise Value!

Ed turned to Steve, and with an equity analysts' impatient demeanor and said, "So, Steve!......**Please proceed to quantify the impact of your five 'Value Drivers' on Enterprise Value, so that I can challenge management and get better information for Shareowners on how management's actions will impact share price!**"

"I'm on it right now, Ed!" said Steve as he shot a brief glance and small smile at Sam that translated as 'We've all experienced this attitude from analysts before!'

"Let me borrow a piece of paper, Ed, and I'll write down the impacts."

Steve continued speaking as he wrote on the paper. "Ed, before you meet with the company, you will undoubtedly do your homework and develop a 'base case' Enterprise Value. In other words, develop your best forecast of the company's Annual Cash Flows and discount them using the company's current WACC (Weighted Average Cost of Capital). In order to make the forecast, you will have assumed certain things in the model about each of the five Value Drivers. For example, you will have assumed a sales growth rate, a percent NOPAT margin, asset use and a capital structure that produces a certain WACC."

"That's right," concurred Ed.

Steve looked at Ed, "Before you visit the company, I am sure that you will compare this 'base case' Enterprise Value to the company's current Market Value (number of outstanding shares x current market price per share). If you see a discrepancy between the two numbers, you will develop ideas and questions to ask management which might help to account for the discrepancy."

Ed nodded, "Yes."

Steve turned back to the coffee table and began writing on a new sheet of paper. "Now, I will share with you some 'rules of thumb' for estimating the impact of changes in the five Value Drivers on Enterprise Value."

Steve continued writing as he spoke. "To develop the 'rules of thumb' we need a base case. My base case will assume that the Enterprise Value is $1,000, and was developed using a 5% growth rate, a 5% NOPAT margin, assets of $1,000, no acquisitions and a WACC of 10%. **"Now remember, I am changing just one 'Value Driver' at a time. The other four are held constant.** Changing more than one Driver at a time would cause them to either compliment or offset one another depending on the direction and magnitude of the changes."

The group edged closer to see the piece of paper.

Steve's piece of paper looked as follows:

"Value Driver"	Unit of Measure	APPROXIMATE Increase in Enterprise Value
1. Sales Growth (Organic Increase in Sales)	1% increase in the annual growth of sales at the same NOPAT margin. OR: Permanent one time 1% increase in Sales at the same NOPAT margin.	5.5% 0.7%
2. Margin Improvement	Permanent 1% increase in NOPAT margin.	11.3%
3. Asset Reduction	A $1 permanent reduction in assets used for a given sales (NOPAT) level.	$1 increase in Enterprise Value for each $1 current reduction of assets.
4. Acquisitions	NPV of the acquired company Enhanced Cash Flows (i.e. including 'synergies') discounted at the acquirer's WACC minus the purchase price.	The impact on the acquirer's Enterprise Value equals the NPV of the Enhanced Cash Flows of the acquired company (discounted at the acquirer's WACC) minus the purchase price.
5. Decreasing the WACC (Weighted Average Cost of Capital)	1% reduction in WACC.	11.5%

Steve pointed to the Sales Growth line. "Let's first assume that management is able to increase the compound annual sales growth by 1% above the 5% growth rate assumed in our 'base case'. In other words, sales growth increases to a rate of 6% p.a. *at constant margins*. The result will be that the net present value—or Enterprise Value—will increase 5.5% from $1,000 to $1,055."

He continued, "On the other hand, *if we only had a one time, 1%, sales increase,*—instead of a compound annual increase—*the answer is different*! For example, if sales increased the first year by 6%, but the compound sales growth remained at 5% every year after that through year 10, then the Enterprise Value would only increase 0.7%, from $1,000 to $1,007.

Everyone nodded indicating that they understood.

Then, looking at Steve's chart, Georgia said, "Let me try the next one to see if I've got it!"

"Go ahead!" encouraged Steve.

Georgia pointed to the line numbered '2' and announced, "If management permanently increases the profit margin by 1%, from 5% to 6%, the Enterprise Value will increase $113, (or 11.3%) from $1,000 to $1,113."

"You've got it!" applauded Steve.

"This isn't so hard!" she said. **"Why don't managers understand this?"**

Steve smiled and said, **"Because schools and society have trained and encouraged managers to think like accountants instead of entrepreneurs!......Managers think *and are paid on accounting EPS* (earnings per share) and with stock options.......Entrepreneurs think cash flow and Economic Profit (EP) and only get paid more if the cash flow increases!"**

He smiled again and returned to the chart this time pointing to line 3 titled 'Asset Reduction'. "If management can sell the same amount of product, but immediately reduce the amount of cash tied up in inventory, receivables or other assets, then, as you will recall from Debra's model, the cash increases the Enterprise Value dollar for dollar. For example, if accounts receivable can be reduced $50 through better collection efforts, it increases cash in the bank by $50 and that immediately increases Enterprise Value by $50 or 5% from $1,000 to $1,050.......BUT, let me emphasize: *Enterprise Value will only improve if the asset is no longer used in the business.* Using Financial Engineering (such as 'Asset Securitization' or operating leases) to make the asset disappear from the GAAP balance sheet, while the company still physically uses the asset, does nothing to improve the net present value of cash flow! For example, in the case of an 'off balance sheet' operating lease, the rent on the operating lease includes an interest component equating to a cost of capital component just as if the assets were on the company's balance sheet!......Accounting gimmicks don't change the cash flow of the business if the asset is still used in the business!......In fact, *because off balance sheet financing typically costs more, cash flow is reduced and this destroys Enterprise Value."*

"Now," continued Steve, "let's turn to arguably the most misunderstood Value Driver: acquisitions!"

"Acquisitions confuse a lot of people, but they are pretty simple!" said Steve. "Just like our 'base case' company, the company being acquired is represented as a set of future cash flows. Those cash flows will be enhanced to include the cash flow resulting from acquisition synergies (e.g. cost savings resulting from combining facilities or administration or new cash flows from increased sales or a new business model—*a.k.a. Enhanced Cash Flow.*) *When that Enhanced Cash Flow is discounted at the acquirer's WACC* (Weighted Average Cost of Capital), *and we subtract the proposed purchase price, we get the net present value (NPV) of the acquisition. This number is the impact on the Acquirer's Enterprise Value.......That's it!......Nothing more!......*

Steve continued discussing acquisitions, "For example, let's suppose that our company wants to acquire a company with sales of $250. We propose to pay $150 for it. However, when we discount the Enhanced Cash Flow (i.e. Annual Cash Flow including synergies) of the proposed acquisition at our 10% WACC, we discover that its Enterprise Value is only $100. If we go ahead and do the acquisition at a $150 purchase price, then the Acquirer will destroy $50 of Enterprise Value [$100 (the present value of the Enhanced Cash Flow of the acquired company) minus $150 (the purchase price of the acquired company)]. The acquirer will end up having only $950 of Enterprise Value after the acquisition—a destruction of $50 of Enterprise Value!"

"Why would anyone pay $150 of cash to get $100 of cash?" asked Tom.

Jose Mendoza, the successful entrepreneur replied, "**Because of reasons such as: failure to understand Economic Profit (EP), being misled by investment bankers, momentum of the deal or 'ego'!**"

"I agree!' said Wendy. "Let's discuss acquisitions in more depth later. But, **I am convinced that a lot of Enterprise Value is being destroyed and a lot of people are being needlessly displaced from jobs because management and Boards do not understand what they are doing!....It's not malicious!....They simply do not understand!**"

Sam's face had a slight frown as he broke a slight smile, but he remained silent.

Steve continued, "The final Value Driver which management can affect is the WACC. Decreasing the WACC discount rate by changing the debt/equity mix of the capital structure or by reducing the after tax cost of debt dramatically improves the Enterprise Value. For example, a reduction of the WACC from 10% to 9%—a 1% nominal reduction— increases the Enterprise Value 11.5% from $1,000 to $1,150." Steve then counseled, "*Be very careful here!* **There has to be a balance between financial risk and business risk.** If you have a lot of business risk in the form of an unproven business model (a'la the dot-coms) or if competition is increasing, don't increase financial risk by materially increasing the debt of the company! Increasing company debt increases the contractual call (promissory notes for principal and interest) which lenders have on the company's cash flow and decreases the company's flexibility exactly when the cash flow may not be realized due to changing business risks."

"Thanks, Steve!" said Ed. "This table containing the 'rules of thumb' puts some real useable substance to your ideas, and gives me a valuable tool!"

"This has been a good discussion," said Jim. "I hope that we can spend more time on acquisitions. Other than the dot-coms, there is nothing in my experience which has burned me and my customers more!"

"Time to eat breakfast!" said Tom.

They all moved energetically toward the Lodge Dining Room.

The Impact of Management's Actions on Enterprise Value:

"Value Driver"	Steve's Comment	Unit of Measure	APPROXIMATE Increase in Enterprise Value
1. Sales Growth (Organic Increase in Sales)	"A sales increase obtained through (1) volume growth, (2) price increases, (3) product mix changes, and/or (4) new business (e.g. new products coming out of research or marketing) will increase Enterprise Value as shown."	1% increase in the **annual** growth of sales at the same NOPAT margin. **OR:**	5.5%
		Permanent one time 1% increase in Sales at the same NOPAT margin.	0.7%
2. Margin Improvement	"NOPAT margins can be improved through absolute reductions in costs, taxes, or through sales increases which absorb fixed costs from other products."	Permanent 1% increase in NOPAT margin.	11.3%
3. Asset Reduction	"Using fewer assets to produce a given level of NOPAT releases cash tied up in those assets."	A $1 permanent reduction in assets used for a given sales (NOPAT) level.	$1 increase in Enterprise Value for each $1 current reduction of assets.
4. Acquisitions	"Acquisitions only increase Enterprise Value of the acquirer by the net present value (using the acquirer's WACC as the discount rate) of the acquired Enhanced Cash Flows (i.e. including 'synergies'), minus the purchase price."	NPV of the acquired company Enhanced Cash Flows (i.e. including 'synergies') discounted at the acquirer's WACC minus the purchase price.	If the NPV of an acquisition's Enhanced Cash Flow (using the acquirer's WACC as the discount rate) minus the purchase price is $1mm, then the acquirer's Enterprise Value will only increase $1 mm.
5. Decreasing the WACC (Weighted Average Cost of Capital)	Decreasing the WACC by increasing the amount of debt or decreasing the after tax borrowing cost of debt, increases the Enterprise Value."	1% reduction in WACC.	11.5%

18.

Cattle!

John Chisholm sat tall in the saddle flanked by six riders.

They looked like they had ridden directly from the Bar 20 out of a Hopalong Cassidy novel by Clarence Mulford or Louis L'Amour (a.k.a. Tex Burns). They were all business and appeared to be as tough as they come. The sun was behind them. It shined directly in Fletcher's eyes. Cattle milled, stirring dust and mooing behind the seven riders.

This was the real West to a ten year old!....Fletcher was ready for it! He and his nine-year-old sister, Emma, had been taking riding lessons with their mom and dad, Nancy and Steve Patterson, since he was 4. He felt as if he could drive these cattle from here to Dodge, if that's what John Chisholm wanted him to do. He knew Emma could do it too! It tugged at him, but he had to admit, Emma was as good a rider as he was—maybe better!

Chisholm began speaking. There were 25 guests present. "We need your help tomorrow in moving our ST Bar herd to better grazing in higher pasture. The range is only ten miles from here as the eagle flies. But, we need to travel a round about way. We'll cover 30 miles in two days, not counting the 20 miles back—part of it steep. When you count chasing the cattle around trees, we'll each cover 60-70 miles round trip.

We'll travel from 9,000 feet in altitude to almost 12,000 feet and back. Along the way we will be nursing 150 head through forests, across rivers and over some dry mesas. It will be hot and occasionally dusty. In the afternoons we will get rained on. But, you won't eat better, and you'll sleep under the prettiest sky that you ever saw........ And you'll have the satisfaction of doing a needed job!......Who's with me?"

Fletcher and Emma's hands shot up first! There wasn't a guest hand that didn't go up!

"Glad to have you along!" said Chisholm. "Today, cowpunchers, we are going to divide you into teams of 5 or 6. You will work with one of the wranglers or drovers who is experienced in handling horses and cattle. You will be with that cowhand for the next 4 days. Today, your drover will teach you techniques for moving cattle as well as some basic penning and cutting skills. Get a good night's sleep tonight! Your team will meet here at 7:30 a.m. sharp tomorrow to start the drive."

"Gina, call out the teams!" As he said this, Chisholm touched his hat with his right hand and neck reined his horse sharp right and loped toward the day's work.

Gina rode forward. "Folks! As I call off your name, go over and introduce yourself to your wrangler. Then, we'll get you mounted and you can practice some new skills."

Gina began calling off the teams.

Fletcher didn't hear his name until the next to last team.

"Barb and Mitch Thompson, Jose and Maria Mendoza and Fletcher and Emma Patterson, you will be teamed with Marianne Robertson.......Go meet and mount up!"

Emma was delighted! She was going to ride along side a real cowgirl!

Fletcher was disappointed. He wasn't going to be riding with one of the cowboys!.......But, that feeling faded quickly as Marianne effortlessly maneuvered her 16.3 hand Paint gelding in front of him, dismounted and strode directly up to him with outstretched hand. Her work worn chink chaps flapped as she walked, and Fletcher caught a glint of sunlight from the rowels on her spurs. A firm handshake from her work strengthened hand, and the way she looked him in the eye from under her 'Boss of the Plains' hat when they shook hands, persuaded Fletcher that she might know a little bit more about cows than he did.

"Fletcher, I am counting on you to get us through to trail's end." she said.

With that, he was ready to follow her. He moved to his horse.

She turned to Emma and said, "I hear that you are an expert rider. I always ride with the best!"

Emma beamed. She just knew this was going to be fun!

As the rest of the guest horses were brought up, Marianne completed introductions to the Mendozas and Thompsons.

When they were mounted, Marianne moved her Paint in front of them and turned him to face them. "You have to know your horse and equipment before you can herd cattle! This morning, we'll let you get more comfortable with your horse, and then I'll introduce you to the equipment you'll be using on the drive."

Marianne continued, "You can't herd cattle if you're sitting on the ground!......**You need to 'sit a deep seat'** if you're going to herd these cantankerous cows, Your horse is occasionally going to be dodging, weaving, starting and stopping to keep these cattle together and moving. If you don't sit the saddle right, you are going to be swallowing dust and looking up at a grinning steer."......

"'Sitting a deep seat' means to sit down in the back of the saddle seat—just in front of the cantle. Let your 'seat bones' feel the saddle, and keep your heels down and your feet in the stirrups in front of you. When your horse is working a cow, add a 'cutter's slump' by relaxing your back and letting it bend a little.......Don't try to get ahead of your horse by leaning forward and standing on the 'balls' of your feet."

She demonstrated.......As she rose and leaned forward, the stirrups swung behind her, and she fell forward onto the saddle horn and began to fall off her horse.......

......Marianne caught herself effortlessly, and said, "That, is a sure way to get the sun in your eyes and be accused of lying down on the job!"

They all laughed.

"There is a secret to every job, and the discipline of 'heels down' and 'sitting a deep seat' is the secret to this one."

Marianne then led them to a large coral at a walk. Once in the coral they began with trotting and loping, then continued limbering up their horsemanship with a little 'pole bending' (weaving around a line of 8 upright poles spaced 25 feet apart) and barrel racing competition . ... The latter, Emma won with ease.

Fletcher's chest swelled with pride in his sister!

At the morning break, they were each outfitted with chaps and large new bandanas. Marianne tied a lariat and small canteen to each saddle and placed a rolled, yellow rider's slicker on top of saddlebags behind each cantle.

It was different riding with all this gear! They took a trail ride to practice dodging bushes that imitated cows. The bushes performed their job well, hooking one canteen, one lariat and two slickers to the ground in the course of an hour.

During lunch of sandwiches under a shady Cottonwood tree, Fletcher and Emma asked Marianne to tell them what cowgirls do on a typical day.

"Occasionally, I wish there was a typical day. But, the rest of the time I'm glad there isn't!" replied Marianne. "We're usually up by 4:30 a.m., saddle our horses and help the wranglers get the guests' horses from the pasture. Then we grain and tack the horses for the guests. When we don't have cattle drives, we ride fence and repair breaks. Sometimes we're helping cattle birth or pulling them out of trouble when they get stuck in a mud hole or tangled in the brush or helping them to get back to the herd when they're lost. There are times when we go after predators killing or causing problems for the herd. Sometimes we cut hay or straw in one of the lower pastures and stack it in barns for winter. We help with shoeing, repair barns, corals and tack. We usually finish up about 9 p.m. and get ready for the next day. I guess you could say that our time is ranch time and our work is ranch work."

"Wow!" said Emma. "If you do all that, what do the cowboys do?"

"They just try to keep up with us cowgirls!"......Marianne smiled teasingly. Then she said more seriously, "On this ranch, we all do what needs doing. Out here it is what you do that counts; it's the talents you bring, and the discipline to get the job done. But also, its what you do when no one is watching!.......And especially what you do in a pinch!......In the end, the only equality that counts is being equal to the task. Out on the range, there isn't anyone but you to see what needs to be done, and there usually isn't anyone but you to do it! If you don't fix something that needs fixed, and a horse or cow gets hurt, you know it's your fault, and I just can't quit a cow or a horse!......Nature doesn't punch a clock!......There were a couple of times in spring when I had to stay out all night in pouring rain to help sick cows or to help them give birth. One night I was out away from the herd found a sick cow down and needing help. I stayed to help. During the night I heard bushes rustling and bark being scratched not too far from my camp. My horse was restless, but I had him staked and hobbled so that he couldn't run away. I made quite a bit of noise as I threw more logs on the fire. Next morning after the cow was up, I herded her back to the ranch. Not too far from camp I passed a dead tree that was covered with claw scratchings and other fresh sign of bear."

Barb shivered. "There must be other things which you could be doing. How much do they pay you?"

"You're right!" said Marianne. "I'm studying to be a veterinarian, and I could have spent time in an air conditioned, small animal practice this summer.......Out here they pay me $40 a day and all I can eat for being smarter than the cattle!........But, how can someone put a value on spending a summer out here!?!".......As she said this, she waved her arm toward the babbling stream in the small valley below and the mountains festooned with garlands of trees, and decorated with facets of sunlight reflecting from the rocks under the clear, blue sky.

"Time to go!" she commanded. "Fletcher, show us how to handle cattle!"

The team spent the afternoon in the coral practicing herding, cutting and penning skills with cattle.

They all did well!…. Especially, Cowboy Fletcher!

PART III

Ghosts in the Trail!

19.

Acquisitions: Just Another Investment!

Sam rose from the supper table as several knives made glasses chime in unison for silence.

"Tomorrow," he began, "some of you will be relaxing, trout fishing, white water rafting or trail riding with our wranglers."........

......"Twenty Five of you will have the responsibility for 150 cattle which help make this ranch possible.......As you drive these cattle to fresh range, you will have the privilege of encountering first hand a small part of the experience that created the legendary American Cowboy!......We won't be swimming swollen rivers or fighting off Commancheros, but you will encounter typical days in the life of a herd.......It's an experience like few others, and it won't be long before even this pale re-creation is a distant memory. **For you cowboys and cowgirls who are going on the drive, say goodbye to your loved ones!.........**"

Sam moved to sit down, and everyone could feel the tension rise in the room......Then, with a big grin, he stood,......and to audible, maternal sighs of relief said,.........**"Until Saturday that is!"**

"We'll see you at the coral in the saddle at 7:30 a.m. sharp tomorrow. Bring your 'necessaries' kit ready to go!"

With that, there was applause, dessert was served, and then, people retired to the Great Room with coffee, hot chocolate and conversation. They broke into small groups. The youngest people including Fletcher, Emma, Nicholas, Jack, Paige and Alexa collected around Chisholm, Dakota, Marianne and Gina to hear about ranch life, and stories of Johnny Appleseed, Pecos Bill, Davy Crockett and Sally Ann Thunder Ann Whirlwind.

Another very special group formed on the couches around the large coffee table where Sam sat.

Barb was the first to speak. "We had a wonderful day today! A person can learn a lot listening to the young people who work here. They have a wisdom learned from the responsibilities of ranch work and the discipline imposed by nature which we should all take to heart."

"True!" nodded Sam with a knowing smile. "You'll learn more from them on the trail during the next few days."

"Sam!" continued Barb, "This morning things were said which made me wonder if my company was doing the right thing. As you have all read in the newspapers, we have made over $1billion of acquisitions over the past year, and we plan to do more. Can we talk more about the issues surrounding acquisitions?"

"I would like that too!" said Wendy.

"I think that it would be useful!" said Jim Perrier. "As I shared with some of you, my brokerage customers have lost the most money when companies have acquired others—ah,…except for the dot com frenzy!…….In fact, I vividly recall a Chicago Tribune article that a friend sent to me in March 2001. The article reported on a study done by a major consulting firm. It said that over 2 and 5 year periods **following a material acquisition or merger, *70 percent* of the acquirers *under performed* their industry peers in stock price appreciation, sales and earnings growth and return on equity (ROE)……**I've read other articles on other studies that put the number between 60 and 70%, but ever since reading that article, **I counsel customers to sell whenever a company announces a major acquisition.......**The odds of its stock price increasing are against them!.........Imagine 70%!.......That's a 70% failure rate in terms of creating Shareowner Value!"

"**You mean acquisitions have a 70% success rate *in destroying Shareowner Value!*"** exclaimed Georgia.

"Right!" said Jim.

"**Why do Board of Directors and management allow that to happen?!?"** asked Debra.

Sam turned. "Steve, why don't you answer Debra's question. This morning you said that acquisitions were one of the five Value Drivers that create Enterprise Value, but you put some conditions on them. How about sharing your thoughts?"

"Glad to!" replied Steve. "I'll preface my remarks with a fundamental rule I learned from experience. **Whenever I have a business problem— especially the tough ones –, I look at the cash flows, and the people who will produce them........**Over time, I have learned that if I get the cash flows and the people right, everything else—including accounting—will work out. But, if I get the cash flows wrong, nothing else seems to matter!"

He continued, "In a minute, I'll apply my rule to evaluating acquisitions.......But, first, let me explain how acquisitions fit in with a company's other investment alternatives."

Barb and others nodded "OK!"

Steve proceeded, "**From a financial perspective, a company is a vehicle which allows the Shareowner to hire industry specialists (managers) to invest and manage cash in a portfolio of operating assets (for example, plants, equipment inventory and receivables, as opposed to financial assets such as bonds, commodities real estate and stocks). These industry operating managers invest the cash along a spectrum of investment alternatives** which looks like this:"

As Steve began writing on a piece of paper he said, "**The objective of investing in any of these alternatives on the Investment Spectrum is just like your personal investing. The objective is to create Economic Profit by earning more than the cost of money being invested**, i.e. in the case of a company, to earn more than the company's WACC (Weighted Average Cost of Capital)."

INVESTMENT SPECTRUM

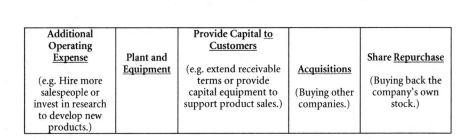

Additional Operating Expense (e.g. Hire more salespeople or invest in research to develop new products.)	Plant and Equipment	Provide Capital to Customers (e.g. extend receivable terms or provide capital equipment to support product sales.)	Acquisitions (Buying other companies.)	Share Repurchase (Buying back the company's own stock.)

Steve continued, "**This Investment Spectrum is a continuum. The boxes I have drawn are meant to be representative, not comprehensive.** Over the course of 3 to 5 years, good management will make investments in every category. When operating managers have cash or additional debt capacity, they will look at the alternatives on this investment continuum and attempt to select the investments which will give Shareowners the greatest return above the company's WACC consistent with the company's goal pyramid."

Steve pointed to the paper, "Beginning on the left end of the Investment Spectrum the alternative uses for cash include investments in:

- **Operating expense** to do things such as hire additional salespeople to grow sales faster or new research to create new products.

- **New plants or equipment** to produce additional product or to produce product more efficiently.

- **New marketing packages** to extend the product life cycles. These packages may use capital to attract people to buy existing products. For example, an automaker might invest cash in financing or leasing vehicles to customers.

- Next, if a company doesn't have enough internal growth options, it may choose to **acquire** other companies. But, again, the return on these investments must be above the WACC if the company is to increase its Enterprise Value.

- Finally, it may find that its best investment option is to acquire its own stock. The company should determine if a **share repurchase** makes sense based upon whether it can acquire its stock below the Enterprise Value per share. If it can, then the cash invested in the share repurchase will earn more than the WACC and create Enterprise Value for the remaining Shareowners."

At this point Steve concluded his comments on the Investment Spectrum and asked the group if there were any questions.

Debra said, "Steve, your Investment Spectrum makes it easy to understand why acquisitions are just another investment alternative for a company, and why they should be evaluated like other investments.......But, does it really happen this way?"

"*And*," added Georgia, "If it really happens this way, why do 70% of acquisitions destroy value for the acquirer?"

Steve looked at Sam and said, "These people are really sharp!"

Sam looked back and said, "That's why I'm letting you explain this!"

The group laughed, and Steve smiled, shaking his head at Sam, as he turned to Debra and Georgia to respond to their questions.

"It's interesting how easily people intellectually understand the Investment Spectrum when it is put in front of them." said Steve. **"When they look at it, they agree that acquisitions belong on the spectrum, and should be evaluated just like any other investment.......And**

they agree that the investment criterion should be that all investments —including acquisitions—have to have a cash flow internal rate of return (IRR) greater than the WACC in order to create Enterprise Value.......But then, something happens........As Jose said this morning, in the pursuit of the deal, hard, cold logic goes out the window and two things enter in........The first is emotion!......The second is the **misguided pursuit of incentives based on accounting EPS or in the belief that higher EPS will increase the value of incentive stock options.**"

Steve continued, "The emotion comes in when CEO's and Boards conclude that they just have to get bigger or best the other bidders in a macho contest........Maybe they just want to keep their jobs because if they don't acquire, the target or other bidders will acquire them!......The way the emotions show up is often subtle. The CEO will almost always have a set of numbers, which indicate that an acquisition will earn a return equal to the WACC......But the numbers include assumptions such as that he can grow the business at 10% p.a. even though prior good management only had a 2% growth rate."

"The incentives come in because **people do what you pay them to do!......If you pay them to increase accounting numbers, they will do that at the expense of cash flow!......This is especially true, if managers believe that the accounting numbers (e.g. EPS) will increase the value of their stock options!**"

"Do people really do this?" asked Georgia.

"Yes!" said Wendy emphatically. "I see companies do it all the time in my M&A work! In my judgment, overpaying for acquisitions is caused more by these two reasons than anything else. They are the principal cause of the 70% failure rate on acquisitions which Jim mentioned."

............There was a thoughtful silence.................

Then Steve said, "Let me make one concluding observation on the Investment Spectrum. Most companies evaluate investments using a discounted cash flow method such as net present value (NPV) or the

Internal Rate of Return (IRR). These are cash flow, *not* GAAP accounting measures. The underlying theory being that the sum of the NPV of all of a company's investments add up to the NPV (or Enterprise Value) of the company...........But somewhere a large majority of CEO's and CFO's loose contact with the logic of cash flow as they look at GAAP EPS and the GAAP impact of acquisitions—both of which drive their incentive plans, and in their opinion, the value of their stock options.....As a result, they force assumptions, they over-pay and destroy Enterprise Value for the Shareowner."

There was a pause in the conversation, and then Sam said, "Steve, thank you! You've given us some good 'straight talk'!"

A COMPANY'S INVESTMENT SPECTRUM

A company is a vehicle that allows the Shareowner to hire industry specialists (managers) to invest and manage cash in a portfolio of operating assets (as opposed to financial assets such as bonds, commodities real estate and stocks). These industry-operating managers invest the cash along a spectrum of investment alternatives.

The objective of investing in any of the alternatives on the Investment Spectrum is to create Economic Profit by earning more than the cost of money being invested, i.e. the WACC (Weighted Average Cost of Capital).

INVESTMENT SPECTRUM

Additional Operating Expense	Plant and Equipment	Provide Capital to Customers	Acquisitions	Share Repurchase
(e.g. Hire more salespeople or invest in research to develop new products.)		(e.g. extend receivable terms or provide capital equipment to support product sales.)	(Buying other companies.)	(Buying back the company's own stock.)

(Note: The boxes on the Investment Spectrum are representative, not comprehensive.)

20.

Most Acquisitions Destroy Value!

Barb spoke, "Steve, the conversation we just had gives me insight into why several members of the group believe that most acquisitions destroy Enterprise Value. But can you now explain how to evaluate an acquisition before the acquisition is approved in order to determine if it creates (or destroys) value?"

"Surely," said Steve......." Let me explain the concept of the valuation, and then I will give you an example."

"Good!" replied Barb.

Steve began, "Recall that over the past several days, we agreed that every company can be represented as a set of cash flows. The value of a company—the Enterprise Value—is the net present value (NPV) of those future cash flows. The discount rate used to calculate the net present value is the WACC (Weighted Average Cost of Capital). The WACC gives both the lenders and the Shareowners a 'fair return' on their capital. Therefore, conceptually, the Enterprise Value is the 'break even' value of the company."

Steve continued, "To evaluate an acquisition using the same discounted cash flow model, we need to make two minor adjustments in order to calculate the acquirer's 'break even' value on the acquired company. First, the discount rate used on the cash flows will be the acquirer's post acquisition WACC. By using the acquirer's post acquisition WACC, the WACC is adjusted to take into consideration the mix of debt and/or equity financing used by the acquirer to finance the acquisition. Second, the cash flows discounted will be the acquired company's cash flows modified to include all cash flow changes in the combined company that result from the combination. These cash flow modifications are often called 'synergies' and include everything which changes cash flow, from a new business model that produces higher sales, to asset reductions, cost savings and margin improvements. The cash flow which includes both the acquired company cash flow and the 'synergies', is called the 'Enhanced Cash Flow.' The Enhanced Cash Flow is what the purchase price is buying."

Steve paused and said, "Let me emphasize one critical fact. The output of the valuation model is only as good as the integrity of the assumptions!......The cash flow from an acquired company is what it is!—it is not what the acquirer wishes ('assumes') it will be! If the acquirer pays too much for the actual cash flow, the acquirer has made an irreversible decision. The acquirer's Shareowners will have to accept a rate of return on that investment below the acquirer's WACC, and therefore, accept the destruction of the acquirer's Enterprise Value through a reduction of share price!"......

Georgia interrupted, "Steve! Do you mean that paying more than the Enterprise Value for an acquisition is just like me paying more than the Enterprise Value when I buy a stock?....Once I've paid too much, I'm stuck with a lower rate of return—a rate lower than a 'fair' return; a rate lower than the WACC!?!"

"Right on!" exclaimed Steve, smiling at a bright lady.

Steve continued, *"To determine how much Enterprise Value is created (or destroyed) for the acquirer's Shareowners, a simple formula applies:"*

Amount of Creation (or Destruction) of Enterprise Value for acquirer's Shareowners	NPV of Enhanced Cash Flows (discounted at the acquirer's post acquisition WACC)	Purchase Price Paid for Acquisition (including assumed debt)
	=	-

"If the purchase price equals the NPV of the Enhanced Cash Flows, then no Enterprise Value is created or destroyed for the acquirer's Shareowners. If the NPV is $21 billion, and exceeds the $20 billion purchase price, then $1 billion of Enterprise Value has been created for the acquirer's Shareowners.......Now, let me show you a more detailed example."

"Wait!" said John. "This helps me to see acquisitions in a different light. Are you saying that when someone announces a $20 billion acquisition, the only real value being created may be 5% of that amount or $1 billion? (i.e. The $21 billion NPV of the Enhanced Cash Flows minus the $20 billion purchase price.)"

"Exactly right!" replied Steve. "In most acquisitions, you are dealing with bright people and investment bankers on both sides of the negotiating table. In a sellers' market such as the past 20 years, there are multiple bidders, and therefore, it is rare if any Enterprise Value is left on the table for the acquirer. That, in part is why 70% of the material acquisitions destroy value for the acquirer's Shareowners."

Steve continued, "Consider all of the risks involved in integrating companies—people, cultural, business, financial, competitive, etc!......All of these have to go right and be on time as assumed for 10 years in order to generate the cash flows which produce the one $1 billion increase in Enterprise Value in the example above. That's a 5% one-time incremental return on a $20 billion investment.......Looked at this way, acquisitions are high risk, low incremental creators of Enterprise Value!"

Steve walked to the chalkboard and erased the day's riding assignments. "I will use the chalkboard to show three cash flows: (1) an Acquirer before an acquisition, (2) the 'Target', and (3) the Acquirer after the acquisition."

As he wrote, Steve spoke, "The first cash flow represents a $10 billion a year sales company with no organic growth in its outlook, but it believes that it can hold margins. For ease, we will assume that its WACC is 10%. As shown, we can calculate its Enterprise Value of $10 billion."

ACQUIRER (Pre Acquisition)

	Total PV	Year 1	Year 2	Year 3	Year 4	Year 5	Year 6	Year 7	Year 8	Year 9	Yea 10
Sales		$10,000	$10,000	$10,000	$10,000	$10,000	$10,000	$10,000	$10,000	$10,000	$10,0
NOPAT		1,000	1,000	1,000	1,000	1,000	1,000	1,000	1,000	1,000	1,00
Annual Cash Flow	$6,140	$1,000	$1,000	$1,000	$1,000	$1,000	$1,000	$1,000	$1,000	$1,000	$1,0●
Terminal Cash Flow	$3,860										$10,0
Cash	$0										
(Debt)	($0)										
PRE ACQUISITION Enterprise Value	$10,000										

"As I said, this company has no growth prospects in its organic business, therefore, management has decided that it wants to acquire other companies to 'increase its growth rate.'"

Steve then began writing a second table. "The Acquirer has identified a Target company which has sales of $1 billion per year with growth projected at 10% per year. For ease, we will assume that as the Target grows, it is increasing the efficiency of its working capital, and that it has excess plant capacity, so that its cash flow increases dollar for dollar with NOPAT. As shown, the Enterprise Value of the Target is $1.8 billion at the Acquirer's 10% WACC."

TARGET COMPANY (Pre Acquisition)

	Total PV	Year 1	Year 2	Year 3	Year 4	Year 5	Year 6	Year 7	Year 8	Year 9	Year 10
Sales		$1,000	$1,110	$1,210	$1,330	$1,460	$1,610	$1,770	$1,950	$2,140	$2,360
NOPAT		100	110	121	133	146	161	177	195	214	236
Annual Cash Flow	$909	$100	$110	$121	$133	$146	$161	$177	$195	$214	$236
Terminal Cash Flow	$909										$2360
Cash	$0										
(Debt)	($0)										
PRE ACQUISITION Enterprise Value	$1,818										

Steve turned to the group. "The Target received multiple bids, and the Acquirer 'won', paying a purchase price of $1.8 billion for the Target. Since there were no synergies (for example, cost reductions by combining operations of the two companies), the Acquirer's cash flow projection (including the Target) after the purchase is shown in the following spreadsheet. *In order to more easily illustrate other points, I have assumed that there was no decrease in the Acquirer's WACC, even though it has $1.8 billion of additional debt.*"

ACQUIRER (Post Acquisition) [Cash Acquisition]

	Total PV	Year 1	Year 2	Year 3	Year 4	Year 5	Year 6	Year 7	Year 8	Year 9	Year 10
Sales		$11,000	$11,110	$11,210	$11,330	$11,460	$11,610	$11,770	$11,950	$12,140	$12,360
NOPAT		1,000	1,111	1,121	1,133	1,146	1,161	1,177	1,195	1,214	1,236
Synergies		0	0	0	0	0	0	0	0	0	0
Annual Cash Flow	$7,049	$1,000	$1,111	$1,121	$1,133	$1,146	$1,161	$1,177	$1,195	$1,214	$1,236
Terminal Cash Flow	$4,769										$12,360
Cash	$0										
(Debt)	($1,818)										
POST QUISITION Enterprise Value	$10,000										

Outstanding shares: 1 billion   Enterprise Value/Share: $10

Steve pointed to the spreadsheet and spoke, "While the present value of the Acquirer's cash flows increased by $1.8 billion, and its sales increased by 10% in the first year, the Enterprise Value did not increase. Reason: the Acquirer had to incur debt of $1.8 billion to make the acquisition, and all of the NPV of the Target's cash flow must go to service the debt.......Nothing is left over for the Acquirer's Shareowners."

"Wow, I never thought of it that way!" said Jim Perrier.

Steve continued, *"There are two yardsticks which can be used to determine if an acquisition creates Enterprise Value for the acquirer.* We already discussed the *first one: The Enterprise Value of the Target company (using the Enhanced Cash Flows) must exceed the purchase price of the Target company.......The second yardstick is that the after tax internal rate of return ('IRR')*—the discount rate equating the Target's Enhanced Annual Cash Flows with the purchase price of the Target— *must exceed the Acquirer's WACC.* When you think about these two measures, you see that they are really two sides of the same coin, and for practical purposes, they result in the same conclusion!"

"Let me ask one more question." said Jim. *"What happens if the Acquirer uses stock instead of cash to buy the Target?"*

"The short answer is that printing stock (i.e. inflating shares out-standing), and diluting existing Shareowners, does not create Shareowner Value," said Steve. "Let me show you."

"In our example we assumed that the Acquirer had to pay Enterprise Value of $1.8 billion for the Target." said Steve. "Let's make the same assumption, but we will assume that the price was paid by issuing additional shares of the Acquirer. As shown here, the post acquisition cash flow of the Acquirer looks exactly the same, except there will be no debt, and the Acquirer's Enterprise Value will go up by $1.8 billion."

ACQUIRER (Post Acquisition) [Stock Acquisition]

	Total PV	Year 1	Year 2	Year 3	Year 4	Year 5	Year 6	Year 7	Year 8	Year 9	Year 10
Sales		$11,000	$11,110	$11,210	$11,330	$11,460	$11,610	$11,770	$11,950	$12,140	$12,360
NOPAT		1,000	1,111	1,121	1,133	1,146	1,161	1,177	1,195	1,214	1,236
Annual Cash Flow	$7,049	$1,000	$1,111	$1,121	$1,133	$1,146	$1,161	$1,177	$1,195	$1,214	$1,236
Terminal Cash Flow	$4,769										$12,360
Cash	$0										
(Debt)	($0)										
POST QUISITION Enterprise Value	$11,818										

Outstanding shares: 1,181,800,000   Enterprise Value/ share: $10

"However, let's assume that originally, the Acquirer had 1 billion shares outstanding and that the Acquirer had an Enterprise Value of $10/ share ($10 billion / 1 billion shares). Since the Enterprise Value of the Target was $1.8 billion the Acquirer had to issue 181.8 million shares at $10 / share (worth $1,818,000,000) to buy the company."

"We can compute the Enterprise Value per share of the combined companies as $11,818 million divided by the 1,181.8 million outstanding shares. In doing this, we see that **the Enterprise Value per share is still only $10, so NO VALUE has been created for the Acquirer's Shareowners even though the acquisition was done with stock.**" concluded Steve.

"Wow!" exclaimed Barb.

"Thanks Steve!" said Sam. Turning to the group he said, "Let's continue this topic with a game!"

Acquisitions will Destroy Enterprise Value unless:

1.

The Internal Rate of Return ('IRR') on the Purchase Price of the Acquired Company

—including synergies—

exceeds the WACC of the Acquirer

OR

2.

The Net Present Value of the Acquired Company
—including synergies—
is Positive!

"These are essentially two sides of the same coin!"

The impact of an acquisition on the Enterprise Value of the Acquirer is equal to the Enterprise Value (including synergies) of the Target company, minus the purchase price.

21.

The Acquisition Game: Illusions of Value!

Sam turned to the group, "As Steve was sharing his insight into the use of cash flows to analyze acquisitions, I thought of a game which might be fun!"

"Great! We could use a little entertainment!....No offense, Steve!" smiled Wendy.

Steve also smiled with a sense of relief as he sat down!

"How do we play the game, Sam?" asked Wendy.

Sam turned toward Wendy. "It's a game which should give us insight into the thought processes that Boards and CEO's use –sometimes intentionally, sometimes naively—to justify many of the value destroying acquisitions which occur daily as Jim cited from The Chicago Tribune and other articles.......The game will also cause us to ask questions Boards should ask if they are attempting to increase Enterprise Value for the Shareowner."

"Let's try it!" said Nancy.

Sam continued, "OK!......Here's how the game works.......Each of us takes a turn volunteering an acquisition rationale which management uses to justify an acquisition. The rest of us are the Board of Directors. **Our job is to state the *key condition* under which the Board is willing to approve the acquisition, so that it will create Enterprise Value for the Shareowners."**

"That's pretty simple!" said Georgia. "Let me try an easy one!"

"Fire away!" said Sam.

Georgia continued. "Management comes to the Board and says, '*We want to do this acquisition because it adds growth!*'"

"I'll respond as a Board member," volunteered Jim Perrier. "*The growth we need is growth in Enterprise Value.* Growth in the form of acquired sales or earnings does not matter if there is no growth in Enterprise Value. You can proceed with the acquisition, if it grows Enterprise Value when you compare the present value of the target discounted at our 10% WACC (Weighted Average Cost of Capital) to the purchase price.......*But, because of the integration risks involved, the increase in the Enterprise Value of our company must be at least 10% of the target's cost.*"

"Excellent!" said Sam. "That's how the game works!......Any questions?......No?......OK, who has the next management rationale for an acquisition?"

John Morgan spoke, "*We want to do this acquisition because it's strategic!*"

Wendy spoke for the Board. "*If its strategic, then the results of the strategy can be expressed in realistic cash flows which can be valued.* **If the resulting calculation does not show an increase in our Enterprise Value, *or if the strategy can't be converted to cash flows*, then the only result of the strategy is to destroy Enterprise Value and you may *not* proceed!**......*Also*, if you elect to present the strategic acquisition, show us the cash flow used in the valuation. These cash flows will be used to judge management's progress in achieving this strategic objective sought with the acquisition, *and* to pay management incentives."

"We want to do this acquisition because there are synergies!" volunteered Mitch Thompson.

"My turn!" said Ed Rogers. *"The only 'synergy' the Board cares about is synergy which increases Enterprise Value.* Therefore, the Board has two conditions prior to proceeding with the acquisition. First, the synergies must be identified and quantified with specific time horizons for achievement. Second, the increase in our company's Enterprise Value derived from the target including synergies (i.e. the Enhanced Cash Flow) must be at least 10% of the target's cost."

"Explain why you included the second requirement." requested Tom Roman.

John responded as if a Board member, "Too often synergies are not realized or are delayed because managers mistakenly believe that they are better managers than the target's management. Also, if we pay away all of the present value of the synergies to the target's Shareowners, we are, so to speak, paying to clean up someone else's problems without any value creation for our own Shareowners in spite of the risk that our management is taking in integrating the companies and in executing the synergies."

"We want to do this acquisition because the acquisition adds earnings!" said Patty Perrier.

Nancy Patterson responded for the Board. "Our criterion is Enterprise Value, not accounting earnings. Therefore, if the present value (using our WACC) of the cash flow associated with generating the additional earnings exceeds the purchase price of the target (i.e. the deal creates positive Enterprise Value), then you may proceed........Frankly, we would like you to create a positive Enterprise Value for our Shareowners equal to at least 10% of the target's cost."

Barb offered a new reason. *"We want to do the acquisition because the deal increases market share!"*

"This one is a real *two edged sword*! I'd like to tackle that for the Board." said Steve.

"Go ahead!" said Ed.

Steve then spoke for the Board. *"Even if market share increases, if it doesn't increase Enterprise Value for the combined company, why take on the integration risks, disruptions and headaches?......*On the other hand, Ms. CEO, if you are saying that you have to do this in order to maintain margins, even though there is no increase in Enterprise Value, then the Board has two questions. *First,* Ms. CEO, what makes you believe that the acquisition will enable you to maintain existing margins? If you cannot, then after the acquisition, the Shareowners will face an even greater absolute deterioration of Enterprise Value than before, because our capital investment is larger! *Second,* in a situation like this, the Board wants the CEO to explain 'Why we aren't the sellers? Why don't we sell our company before declines in margins further deteriorate our cash flow, and therefore, our Enterprise Value?'"

"The acquisition reduces our WACC (Weighted Average Cost of Capital—the discount rate)!" volunteered Wendy.

Debra offered Board comments. "Ms CEO, *if the deal does nothing more than change our WACC by increasing leverage, then you may **NOT** proceed. There are other less risky alternatives.* At the next Board meeting, the Board wants to see a proposal for repurchasing the company's own stock including a calculation of the company's current Enterprise Value per share vs. its current stock price. The analysis should evaluate refinancing existing debt to see if its after tax cost can be reduced, therefore, reducing the WACC. We also need to see an analysis showing the impact on WACC and the AFTER TAX impact on Shareowners of a large, one time, cash dividend paid with borrowed money."

"'The acquisition helps us to diversify.' or 'The acquisition helps us to build a new business model.'" stated Jose.

"I've seen the equity analysts and management praise this one to my customers before with disastrous results!" said Jim. "As a Board member, here is how I would respond, 'First, explain why this is the right market to diversify into?'......Then, we get into the acquisition details......'What is the current market price of the target, the current Enterprise Value of the target and the price you are proposing to pay for the target? *If you are proposing to pay a price above the current market price, please explain why the average Shareowner can't diversify more cheaply just by buying the shares of the target in the market?*....If you are proposing to pay a premium to the Market Value because of a 'new business model', then show me the net present value of the incremental cash flow from the new business model —if any—which exceeds the acquisition cost and, therefore, rewards our Shareowners for taking the risk of creating the new business model.'"

"Let's take one last illusion," said Sam.

"*The acquisition creates Shareowner Value!*" offered Barb.

Ed responded with analytical brevity. "Prove it! Show the Board why and how much the Enterprise Value increases!"

The group laughed, and applauded!

"Spoken like a statesman, Ed!" said Sam.

Sam continued, "Let me emphasize two conclusions which come out of your collective comments. *First,* **an acquisition should never be approved without a realistic cash flow projection,** which both demonstrates the creation of Enterprise Value, and can serve as the basis to *judge and pay* management actions post acquisition. Companies require cash flows showing creation of net present value on other investments, such as plants; acquisitions should be no different! *Second,* **whether acquisitions are made for cash or stock, if the acquirer pays too much it's a bad acquisition.**......*It's no different than when an individual buys a stock.* Once the acquirer pays more than the present value of the Enhanced Cash Flows, there is nothing to do but take a loss as the acquirer's Enterprise Value declines and regresses to the new net present value of cash flow, ...or the acquirer can hope to find a greater fool to buy the target from it at a higher price. Once you cut through the hype, it's as basic as that.......All water seeks its own level!"

"Thanks for introducing us to this game, Sam! This would be a good game to use in training my management!" said Barb. "What do you call it?"

Sam's eyes twinkled. "I call it 'The Acquisition Game: Illusions of Value.'"

The Acid Test of a proposed Acquisition is:
Does it increase the Acquirer's Enterprise Value?

People who cannot produce the numbers,
or who do not understand them
often use the following 'illusions'
to argue their case:

It adds Growth!

It's Strategic!

There are Synergies!

It adds Earnings (or Sales)!

It increases Market Share!

It reduces our WACC!

It helps us Diversify!

It helps us build a New Business Model!
It creates Shareowner Value!

Causing people to put their visions (or illusions) into cash flow,
either proves or disproves their argument on paper,
but in either case,
if the acquisition proceeds,
the forecast cash flow provides a benchmark
for measuring later actions,
and as a basis for paying incentives to managers!

22.

Other Illusions of Value!

Debra used the break in the conversation to make an observation, "There are other actions unrelated to acquisitions which cause the illusion of creating Enterprise Value, and I think that we need to do a better job of making Shareowners aware of them."

"How about sharing some of them with us?" asked Sam.

"**Share splits!**" responded Debra.

She continued. "When I cut an apple pie into 10 pieces, I still only have one pie..........Enterprise Value is the value of the firm whether one share or ten million shares are outstanding. The number of shares does not change the company's cash flows, or the WACC (Weighted Average Cost of Capital)!......While some may interpret the announcement of a stock split as affirming growth prospects, it does nothing to realize them. In fact, as in the case of the dot coms, the stocks were often split just to make them 'more affordable' even though the Market Value far exceeded the Enterprise Value.

"How about other actions which cause illusions of creating Shareowner Value?" asked Sam.

"**Dividends!**" replied Debra. "If I take a piece of the apple pie and hand it to the Shareowner, there is still only one pie and there are still only 10 pieces of that one pie……….. Dividends are merely a transfer of cash from the company to Shareowners. In our earlier discussion of Shareowner Value, we said that Shareowner Value is the sum of the Market Value plus the dividends. (Let's assume the Market Value and the Enterprise Value are in equilibrium.) The dividend reduces the firm's Enterprise Value by $1mm, but since the Shareowner's portfolio money market account increases by that $1 million, there is no creation or destruction of the Shareowner's Value…..Again, dividends may be viewed as affirming a company's growth rate, but in and of themselves, dividends do not alter Enterprise or Shareowner Value!"

"'**Non recurring—one time' charge-offs** bother me," said Steve. "First, individual companies are taking these charge-offs more frequently—*in some cases every quarter. So, in reality, these companies are not recognizing ongoing costs of renewing the business, and are, therefore, routinely overstating income.* The second illusory aspect of these charge-offs is increased earnings…….Higher reported earnings after the charge-off should not fool people! Often the improvement is merely due to the fact that depreciation and amortization related to the charged-off assets no longer 'hit' the income statement…….BUT, neither Economic Profit nor Enterprise Value increase as a result of the charge. The reasons: cash flow doesn't increase, *and* capital (debt plus Market Value of equity) invested in the business doesn't change. The capital was already spent, and the charge-off doesn't get it back!"……

"A problem related to one time charge-offs is '**non recurring gains**'," said Debra.

"You're right!" said Steve. "Companies often slip items like asset sales or gains from one time events such as legal settlements into net income without minimal comment to Shareowners. Often Shareowners miss the fact that they should not expect these gains in the future. As a result they build future growth projections off an illegitimate base."

"An especially deceptive set of nonrecurring gains relates to **divestitures**," volunteered Wendy.

"How so?" asked Mitch.

Wendy replied, "They are problematic for two reasons. First, they are *non*-recurring, and, as Steve said, Shareowners should not build them into future growth expectations. Second, management may do divestitures to generate GAAP gains when in fact they destroy Enterprise Value."

"How do divestitures which generate GAAP gains destroy Enterprise Value?" asked Barb.

Wendy responded, "When the divestiture occurs, the company reports a GAAP gain on the income statement because the historic book value of the divested company is small. Reason: the book value of the divested company has been depreciated and charged to earnings over prior years. However, if the *after tax* cash received for the divested company is below the Enterprise Value of the divested company, there has actually been a destruction of Enterprise Value!"......

"A brief example may help," volunteered Steve.

"Please go ahead and give one," said Wendy.

Steve began, "O.K.......Let's assume that a $1,000 divestiture occurs, and that the divested company's book value had been written down over prior years to $0. That means the Seller will report a $1,000 pre-tax gain ($650 after tax-assuming a 35% tax rate.) on its GAAP income statement. However, from a cash flow perspective instead of owning the divested company and earning the 10% WACC on its $1,000 Enterprise Value, the seller is left with only $650 ($1,000 minus $350 of taxes) to invest at the 10% WACC. That's an immediate destruction of $350 of seller Enterprise Value at the time of the divestiture!"

"Unbelievable!" exclaimed Barb. "I hadn't thought of that!...I understand what you mean, and you're right!"

"Another illusion is **share repurchases done at a price above the Enterprise Value per share.**" said Wendy......"Repurchasing stock at a price above Enterprise Value per share can increase accounting EPS by reducing outstanding shares. BUT, it destroys Enterprise Value in the same way as making an acquisition at a price above the Target's Enterprise Value (including synergies). *When a company repurchases its own shares, it is acquiring itself and the same valuation rules apply as to third party acquisitions—except that it is acquiring a known entity, and there is no integration risk."*

"**Increasing stock price with no corresponding increase in Enterprise Value** is another illusion of value creation," said Ed. "Momentum investors keep putting money into a stock as its price goes up, (or sell, as the price goes down). The price movement occurs regardless of any change in Enterprise Value."

"Excellent point!" said Wendy.

There was a pause.

"Well, it has been a long day." said Sam. "With time, I am sure that we could name many other illusions of value which temporarily impact GAAP earnings or stock price, but do not change Enterprise Value.......**The images of easy money and 'growth' from acquisitions are like mirages or ghosts in the desert.......After you invest precious time and energy chasing the ghost and his gold, the apparition quickly disappears, and you are left with the reality of sore feet, empty pockets and unsatisfied thirst!**......Focusing on realistic cash flows and earning WACC helps to minimize the chance of being fooled by events or announcements having no real cash impact on the company."......

"Get a good night's sleep!......I'll see you for coffee or at the coral in the morning!"

*Illusions of creating Shareowner Value
are many, and
will change over time!*

The surest way to avoid illusions......

*......is to evaluate a company and its actions
based on their impact on Enterprise Value
—the net present value of realistic cash flow!*

PART IV

*Of Old Trail Bosses
And
Lead Steers.*

23.

Lessons from the Old Trail Bosses!

Attendance at morning coffee was light on Wednesday.

As Barb and Mitch Thompson commented on this, Wendy observed that a lot of people were probably still assembling their 'necessaries' kits for the cattle drive.

The porch was peaceful and the group reflective..........

Jose Mendoza especially seemed lost in thought.

"Jose!" said Barb, "You shouldn't be doing such serious thinking on vacation!"

"Ah, I'm not thinking, just reflecting." said Jose.

"Care to share?" she asked.

"Mmmm.......I was reflecting on today's cattle drive," replied Jose......."And, remembering stories about my great grandfather, who was a vaquero in Texas after the Civil War."

"Really!!?" said Wendy. "Tell us about him!"

The group could see Jose's pride as he spoke.

"Well,......my thoughts are as much about his participation in building the American Cowboy legend as they are particular to my grandfather." he replied......."You know, after the Civil War, times were hard. Men fresh out of the armies had no homes and needed work.

Texas had millions of longhorns roaming wild, and people back East were hungry. So, tough, hardy men migrated to Texas and the great cattle drives north to the Kansas railheads began in earnest. I have heard it estimated that in the 15 year period after the Civil War over 10 million cattle were driven north from Texas to the railroads."

"My great grandfather was anxious for adventure. He had herded cattle on ranches in Mexico, but he was restless to see more and to make more, so he moved north. Over the years, he signed on with many of the tough cattle outfits, and eventually became a Trail Boss. In the 1860's—80's these types of cowboy outfits drove individual herds of 2,500—10,000 cattle over the Shawnee, Chisholm, Western and Goodnight-Loving Cattle Trails—to name a few........From stories of my great grandfather, I learned, that each of these cattle drives was a unique experience;......a fight for survival with man or nature—usually both—from Commancheros to draught, from rustlers to bitter cold. The drives always required courage, innovation, self-reliance and self-discipline from every member of the drive in order to prevail over constantly changing circumstances........The stories I remember included a famous Texas Longhorn, by the name of 'Old Blue'. 'Old Blue' was special! The cowboys used to take that old steer back and forth over the 1,000-mile trail between the Texas ranges and the Kansas railheads. The reason 'Old Blue' wasn't sold as steak was that he was too valuable to the Trail Bosses. They would put 'Old Blue' at the front of the Texas herd, and all the cows would follow him up the trail to Kansas. He was the lead steer. He got the herd moving quickly at the beginning of the day and kept them moving at the right pace in the right direction all day. It was a lot easier and took fewer men when they had a steer *leading* the herd up the trail *compared to driving* the herd up the trail."

"Wow!" said Wendy. "Your great grandfather was one of the real cowboys! That's quite a heritage to share with your grandchildren."

"Yes," said Jose, "and the curious part is that even today those stories are teaching me new things that I will share with my children."

"Like what?" asked Wendy.

"Well......." he replied. "When I first sat down this morning, it quickly flashed through my mind that during the past few days, we have discussed definitions of value and illusions of value, but we haven't talked about *what actually causes value to happen.* And then, as I was reflecting on my great grandfather, it occurred to me that those Old Trail Bosses knew something about making value happen that would benefit us!"

"How's that?" asked Mitch in a surprised voice.

"Think about it!" Jose exhorted. "Those old Trail Bosses made value happen out of thin air with sheer will power! They started with nothing but their own ability and the most difficult circumstances conceivable.......Imagine!!!" Jose waived his arms indicating the vast loneliness of the South and West Texas plains........."These Trail Bosses went into the most unforgiving country with rough, often downright salty men and a dream to find and drive cattle north. Together, they fought thirst, storms, stampedes, rustlers, Indians, lack of sleep and ate dust for 110 days at a time. The Trail Bosses got these men—cowboys—to 'ride for the brand', and to risk their lives for $30 a month—paid at trail's end.......How did they do it?"

Jose paused, then continued, "As I reflected, it occurred to me that driving 10 million cattle to the railroads didn't happen by luck. Many of these successful Trail Bosses and their cattle drives had some common secrets."........

In a soft voice, Barb queried, "What do you think they were?"

Jose turned and said, "I can only guess,......but, I think that their secrets were something like this........*First*, the Trail Boss was 'loyal to the brand;' and he was committed to completing the drive no matter how difficult. In many cases, overcoming the obstacles and completing the drive wasn't just about money;…it was about pride in doing the job or in keeping his word.......*Second*, he made sure that everyone knew their trail's end goal: it was to reach a certain town at trail's end,—such as Abilene or Dodge City or Wichita—*with the cattle*........*Third* among his crew, the Trail Boss encouraged a culture of finding ways to overcome any obstacle in achieving their trail's end goal. ....*Fourth*, they had a lead steer to keep everyone—including the cows and cowboys-focused on moving in the right direction at the right pace each and every day;.........and, *finally*, they knew they would get paid well, but only if they delivered the beef at trail's end!"

"Jose, I think you've made an excellent read of the Trail Bosses!" said Sam. "As you said, their recurring success was no accident!"......

"Jose," asked Barb. "Can you translate these lessons from the old Trail Bosses into contemporary action? **What can I do to *cause value* to happen in my company?**"

"I will try!" he responded......."Over the years. I have done things to make my company successful, and they parallel the lessons from the old cattle drives. I think I would translate the lessons for a present day audience as follows."......

"*First*, the CEO, must be personally and completely committed to 'Riding for the Brand' and to achieving the trail's end goal of creating Enterprise Value each and every day."......

"*Second*, the CEO must tell people that they are going to Dodge City with the entire herd!......In modern terms, *the CEO must* not only *communicate the company's goal pyramid*, but he must *train* the people—indoctrinate them in it! *The top of that goal pyramid must be 'Creation of Enterprise Value'*! **It is striving for that single goal which empowers people's creativity and causes constant renewal and reinvention to overcome obstacles—**......no matter what obstacle which arises along the trail."......

"Permit me a side observation," he said. "While the goal of creating Enterprise Value empowers long term creativity among employees, it is Leadership which inspires it...... Greatness requires both!"

Jose then continued with lessons learned from the old Trail Bosses.

"*Third*, to achieve the goal of constantly increasing Enterprise Value, **the CEO must change the company's culture to a culture which causes constant renewal and reinvention in the pursuit of creating Enterprise Value. This type of culture is essential if the company is to adapt, survive and prosper in a constantly changing, and very hostile landscape**.......I think that these last two lessons are very dependant on each other!........... The people in the company must feel the CEO's full, unwavering commitment to both the trail's end goal and to the new culture. The CEO must breathe it, eat it and sleep it. ....Like the old Trail boss, the CEO must ride for the brand in actions, not just words.......He must be sincere about it! If the CEO isn't sincere about it, and won't bet his career to achieve it, others will not take risks for it, and the CEO will fail. Everything needs champions, and living the culture is something that the Trail Boss must do him or her self!"

"*Fourth*, there must be a 'Lead Steer'—a simple, unequivocal, tangible mechanism which people can use as their compass each day to make decisions which will create Enterprise Value. My Lead Steer has been Economic Profit ('EP') or as many call it, 'EVA.'"

"*Finally*, pay must be linked directly to Enterprise Value. **People should get paid when they get the cattle to Dodge.** There can be no confusion or conflict between incentive plan goals. People should get paid good incentives, but *only* if they create Enterprise Value........*Stop using stock options as a primary incentive*!!!.......**Stock options are like paying people based upon the price of cattle in Dodge, rather than whether they get the cattle to Dodge!**..........Managers should be paid for what they control—Enterprise Value......not a by-product—stock price—which includes the vagaries of supply and demand!!"

"You woke Mitch up with that one!!!" laughed Barb.

"How do you know that these things cause value to happen?" asked Debra.

"They worked for me," said Jose. "And, when I walk into companies who are not growing or not increasing Enterprise Value, I see their absence."

Lessons Learned from Old Trail Bosses

1.

'Loyalty to the Brand' begins at the Top!
The Trail Boss must be totally and sincerely committed to
'Riding for the Brand'
and to achieving the trail's end goal,
or others won't follow!

2.

Communicate the trail's end goal of creating Enterprise Value to
everyone.
However, recognize that while 'working' the goal empowers creativity,
it is Leadership that inspires it!

3.

The Trail Boss must cause a culture of renewal and reinvention in order for the crew to overcome obstacles in the constantly changing, hostile route to trail's end!

4.

Have a Lead Steer—A visible compass, like Economic Profit ('EP')— which people can use daily to keep them on course to the goal.

5.

*Pay people well
When...
they deliver the beef!
at trail's end!*

24.

Pyramids in West Texas!

"Jose!" said Barb. "If I listened well, you think that **a key lesson to be learned from the Trail Bosses, is that CEO's must create and foster a culture which causes the company to continuously reinvent and renew itself so that it can adapt to a constantly changing competitive landscape.**"

"That's right!" said Jose. "That's the only way the company can survive! **The culture must cause the company to continuously reinvent itself.** *The culture must foster constant evolution—not periodic, debilitating revolution.*"

"But how do I do that?" Barb asked.

"You build a pyramid!" he replied.

"A pyramid?!?" said Wendy.......... "In Texas?"

"Please, allow me some poetic license!" Jose pleaded as he laughed. "After all, I got the idea from my salespeople!"......

"Your salespeople!" said Debra as she piled on.

"It is so nice to be in the bosom of a sympathetic audience!" he laughed......... "Here is how it happened."

"In the mid 1980's when the US was going through what the economists were calling a 'rolling recession', my company was having difficult times. In fact it felt like the recession was rolling right over us! I started asking myself the trail's end question. 'Why am I in business?'"......

Jose looked at Wendy. "I thought about the question for several weeks,.......Since my salespeople used 'sales pyramids' to help them define selling priorities, I took to drawing 'goal pyramids' to help me visualize my company's goal priorities.....I finally concluded that my company's goal pyramid looked like this."

Jose sketched his company's Goal Pyramid on a napkin.

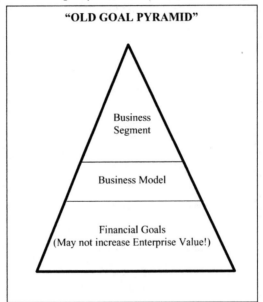

"My company's old primary goal was to make plastic fasteners for the automotive industry, using a low cost, low margin, commodity business model. I felt that by doing this we could meet the company's financial goals of increasing sales 10% p.a., earning a 5% after tax profit, and generating a 15% return on the book equity.......I *assumed* that by being in a business segment with a particular business model, the company would achieve its financial goals."

"Well," said Jose, "As the company's market share increased to about 35% in the mid 80's, I discovered that growth almost stopped, and margins narrowed."

"About this time, the newspapers reported on several major firms having trouble with their stock prices. It seems that they—like my company—had not evolved their business strategy and business models in response to changing markets and market share.......Very fortunately, as I was going through this soul searching, a friend invited me to join her in attending a seminar on EVA (Economic Value Added) hosted by Stern Stewart,......after which, I read several books on Economic Profit written by others."

"The following Sunday as I sat in my backyard, it occurred to me that maybe companies weren't in trouble because of bad business strategies or defective business models! After all, smart people ran these companies.......Maybe their problems were caused by poor priorities in their company's Goal Pyramid;......maybe their goal priorities prevented them from adapting—or adapting fast enough—to a changing environment."

"Then it *really* came to me!" exclaimed Jose. "I finally put the key ideas together!"

"I realized that the primary—dare I say 'primal'—goal of any company is to survive—to stay in business!"

"To earn the right to stay in business, a company must continually create Enterprise Value. It is the creation of Enterprise Value that evidences that the company is satisfying its constituents: customers, employees, communities, suppliers and Shareowners; it is the creation of Enterprise Value that justifies a company's existence.......So, I redrew my company's Goal Pyramid, and put 'first things, first.' I put creation of Enterprise Value at the top."

Jose sketched a new pyramid.

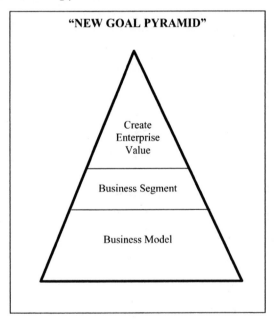

"That's a great visual image," said Barb. "People can quickly see the company's priorities."

"Yes," said Jose. "But, once I saw the New Goal Pyramid, I realized that I was about to embark on changing the culture of my company.......It was going to be like putting the Quality Process in place!......It had to start from the CEO down or it wouldn't work!.......I still wanted employees to do all the important things such as customer satisfaction, employee satisfaction and quality. But, I wanted them to understand why they were doing it, and what needed to be done to earn the right to stay in business. I also wanted the culture to empower and reward them to create Enterprise Value."

"That's a tall order!" said Mitch.

"And if I was going to be successful, I knew that I needed a lead steer!" said Jose

*When a Company
makes
creation of Enterprise Value
its primary Goal,......*

*it results in a cultural change
that causes the company
to continuously renew and reinvent itself
in order to adapt
to a changing environment.*

*A company has to reinvent itself
in order to increase Enterprise Value
every year!*

25.

The Lead Steer!

Debra overheard Jose's last comment as she walked back to the morning discussion and handed him a second cup of coffee. She asked, "Jose, please explain this idea of a Lead Steer?"

After thanking her for the coffee, with feigned surprise he said, "Why,…the idea of a Lead Steer is fundamental to leading people as well as to moving cattle!"

With an annoyed tone in his voice, John said, "What do you mean by that?"

Jose smiled, and with obvious tongue in cheek, he replied, "I once read that a 'semi-fictional' Trail Boss by the name of Jim Flood was telling his cowboys their duties before a drive. Jim said,

> Boys, the secret of trailing cattle is never to let the herd know that they are under restraint. Let everything that is done be done voluntarily by the cattle.……

Jose continued, "While I don't consider people to be cattle, I do think that people and cattle have a few things in common. One is that both people and cattle are more enthusiastic when they think that they are in control, and they think that something is their own idea!"

John bought into Jose's good-natured approach, and chuckling said, "I'll buy that!"

Jose continued, "Everyone on a cattle drive knows and 'buys in to' the fact that we're headed to Dodge City! But when we're in the middle of a West Texas plain surrounded by loneliness, its helpful to have a compass to tell us which direction to go. And its important to have a Lead Steer to get everyone moving together in the right direction at a pace which still leaves some beef on the cows when they arrive in Dodge!"

Sam sat back and chuckled quietly to himself as he saw amazed looks on the faces of the group. He knew that Jose was right on the money, and long on tales!

"Once I knew that the goal pyramid was going to cause a cultural change, I needed a simple, powerful tool to keep people focused.—a tool which they could use minute by minute to make decisions while they were 'in the saddle and on the move'.......I knew that physically I couldn't make all the decisions on the trail; perhaps more importantly, I knew that I wasn't smart enough to make all of them! So, I had to find a way to delegate—to empower—the people on the company's front lines, so that they would have a high probability of making decisions in the same way that Shareowners would make them. The Lead Steer needed to be simple so that people would be comfortable using it, yet elegant enough so that it captured the important factors in a decision."

"In one sense, you needed a Swiss Army knife!" said Tom..."Something that can fix whatever problem comes up!"

"Good analogy, Tom!" said Jose. "I needed a simple, universal tool to put in front of people so they could take queues from it just the way they would take queues from a lead steer as it moves up the trail at a steady pace."

"As I searched for my Lead Steer, I finally found it in the form of the formula for Economic Profit (EP)."

Jose scribbled the Economic Profit formula that they had seen previously on a napkin.

Jose continued, "As Tom said, this formula is like a Swiss Army knife. Using it is almost intuitive! A person can use it 'on his feet' to resolve issues of value creation as they arise day to day in real time. The formula simply says that in order to create value, you need to earn more than the cost of your capital. It also gives the user the cost of capital in dollar terms.......These are easy things that everyone can understand."

$$\text{Economic Profit (or 'EP')} = \text{Net Operating Profit after Tax (NOPAT)} - (\text{Capital} \times \text{WACC})$$

Jose pointed at the EP formula, "**When you study the formula, you notice that it encompasses all of the resources needed to produce and sell a product, and it tells you if you are creating economic value using them!**......For example, Net Operating Profit After Tax ('NOPAT') includes the impact of sales and product mix changes on income as well as changes in costs—including people costs. 'Capital' includes every asset needed in making and selling the product from equipment to receivables and inventory. The WACC capital charge shows that capital has a cost and what that cost is.......**The EP formula enables the average person to see the direct trade-off between an extra dollar of expense in the income statement versus an extra dollar of capital spent to solve a problem.**"

Jose became even more excited, and sat on the edge of his chair as he sketched some brackets below his EP formula.

$$
\begin{array}{ccccc}
\text{Economic} & & \text{Net} & & \\
\text{Profit (or 'EP')} & = & \text{Operating} & - & \text{(Capital x WACC)} \\
& & \text{Profit after} & & \\
& & \text{Tax} & & \\
& & \text{(NOPAT)} & & \\
\end{array}
$$

COMPASS

"If you are 'in to' navigation," he said, "you will notice a wonderful analogy in what I am about to say!......Most companies use some form of income statement measure to judge their real time performance. That's like using a compass.......It tells you direction, but it doesn't tell you where you are or what progress you are making!......Even when a company adds ratios like Return on Capital Employed (ROCE)[6], the ratios are very difficult for most people to use. For example, it is difficult for people to use ratios to determine the tradeoff between an extra 1% of ROCE and $1,000 of expense—especially when they are in the 'heat of battle'. Even if people could easily relate the ratios to absolute dollars of investment or expense, the ratios don't tell them if their actions are creating Enterprise Value or how much!"

"Look at the Economic Profit formula!" Jose pointed. "Not only does it tell you direction—like a compass—but it tells you your position with respect to the use of capital, AND whether your actions are creating Economic Profit which is my proxy for Enterprise Value. To draw an analogy with navigation, Economic Profit is the financial equivalent of a Global Positioning System ('GPS'); it gives you your precise position

---

6. Return on Capital Employed (ROCE) is often defined as: Net Income / (Debt + Book Value of Shareowner's Equity).

with respect to the creation (or destruction) of economic value. When you look at your exact position (i.e. your latitude and longitude) at two different points in time you can see if you are making progress toward your destination: the goal of creating Enterprise Value!"

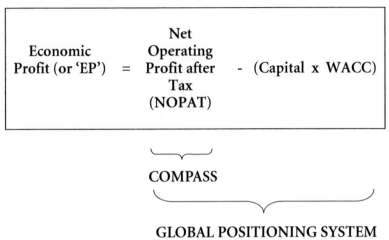

Jose began sketching again, although this time it was to draw an inverted pyramid. "Let me show you why I am so excited about the elegant simplicity of the Economic Profit formula and its Global Positioning capability especially in terms of telling the person on the front lines if his or her decision is creating Enterprise Value."

He pointed to his new sketch, "I call this inverted pyramid the "Product Life Cycle Pyramid".

"A business—or a product line—usually starts out at the bottom of the Product Life Cycle Pyramid with a single unique product or service. As a result, the 'Product' commands an acceptable NOPAT (Net Operating Profit After Tax) and creates Enterprise Value."

'PRODUCT LIFE CYCLE PYRAMID'

'Product Supreme'

'Product Plus'

Product

"However, soon competition appears. As a result, to continue creating Enterprise Value, the company must move its Product offering up the pyramid and in the process must create 'Product Plus'. This is the original Product bundled with enhancements such as extended credit terms, or additional service or 'free' options."

Jose shook his head, "But eventually the competition catches on and now the company has to create 'Product Supreme.' This product offering occurs later in the product life cycle and bundles additional 'free' options or service such as extended warranties or capital equipment and term financing with the Product."

He continued, "The exact elements in the inverted pyramid will vary depending on the product or company. But one thing will not. As companies take increased market share or as products go through life cycles, they all evolve up the pyramid. As a result, companies must manage:

- high margin and low margin businesses, and
- high capital and low capital businesses

side by side."

Jose looked around, "Until I used Economic Profit, I couldn't tell whether one division or one product line was better than another. The hodgepodge of infinite possibilities made it impossible for me to tell which division or product was a good or bad performer in creating value from one year to the next!..........Now, my people and I just look to see if the business is (1) creating a positive Economic Profit in dollar terms and (2) increasing the dollars of EP ($ EP) each year."

"The combination of the Goal Pyramid and the Lead Steer is critical. In a competitive market place, you have to constantly renew and reinvent—to constantly change the products and services you are offering to the customer. The requirement of increasing the amount of $ EP each year forces you to constantly renew and reinvent. BUT, it also keeps the inverted Life Cycle Pyramid balanced so that you don't deceive yourself by investing too much capital or reducing margins to the point that you are destroying Enterprise Value in the process of reinventing product offerings."

"Sorry for this monologue!" said Jose apologetically, "But let me make one last point."

"To me a great hidden power of Economic Profit is that it is mathematically linked to Enterprise Value—the net present value of cash flow[7]. Don't worry; I won't attempt to prove it! But, the result is that if a company increases its $ EP each year, it will increase its Enterprise Value....That is my focus for the company each year—a known $ improvement in EP. It is very easy for everyone in the company to understand and to contribute to...........The formula for Economic Profit and the related $ improvement in EP each year are my Lead Steer—my 'Old Blue'!" concluded Jose.

"Jose, I think that there is another significant hidden secret of Economic Profit as a lead steer," said Steve.

"What's that?" asked Jose.

---

7. The present value of EP discounted at the WACC plus the starting capital equals the Enterprise Value.

"When operating managers use the formula for Economic Profit to think about how they sell their products, they think differently and more aggressively." Steve replied.

"How so?" inquired Debra.

"When a person thinks about a goal of achieving a certain margin on their product, they think one dimensionally. They think about getting that margin on their book of business and they walk away from sales which won't get them the margin." said Steve. "A person who is working on an Economic Profit incentive plan will look at that sale in terms of the capital tied up in inventory and receivables to make the sale. As long as s/he can get a positive Economic Profit and earn more than the cost of capital on that sale, s/he will make the sale, even if it must be made at a lower margin.......People who are trained to use Economic Profit become better business people, and it changes the way that they compete. Economic Profit really alters the competitive dynamics of an industry in favor of the company that uses it!"

Steve continued, "Properly managed, the requirement of increasing $ EP each year, causes a company to penetrate global markets quickly, gradually obsolete its own product, and develop new products which in this context is what renewal is all about."

There was a brief pause, then Barb said, "My thanks to both Jose and Steve for sharing! You have given us some really important ideas to think about as we ride during the next two days! I hadn't thought about the fact that changing a financial goal could change the way a company or industry competes!"

"You're right!" said Wendy, "I hadn't considered it either, but it's a powerful idea!"

"And I still would like to talk more about stock options and incentive plans!" reminded Mitch.

"Well, I see the cook at the door, and I'm just looking forward to eating!" said Tom.

"Let's go get it!" seconded Sam.

Economic Profit (or 'EP')
is a powerful lead steer because:

1.

The formula encompasses the cost and benefit of all the
resources required to produce a product or service.

2.

The formula makes it easy for people to understand the
tradeoff between a dollar of operating income (or expense)
and the cost of a dollar of capital required to produce it.

3.

The formula makes it easy to understand that a company needs to earn more than its cost of capital, or no value is created.

4.

The formula makes it easy to set dollar goals for increasing EP which translate to increases in Enterprise Value—the net present value of cash flow.

Economic Profit (or 'EP')	=	Net Operating Profit after Tax (NOPAT)	- (Capital x WACC)

26.

'Head 'em up!..........Move 'em out!'

Everyone was on time......in fact early!

By 7:30 the guests were all mounted and in two semi-circular rows facing the Trail Boss and his crew.

Sam, mounted on a handsome Appaloosa gelding named War Bonnet, sat straight as he spoke. "Welcome to the ST Bar trail drive. I'll be your Trail Boss on this drive. We are counting on you and to get these cattle up to Sweet Pasture where the cattle will graze for the next two months. Let me make some introductions."

As Sam introduced them, the crew tipped their hats. "Our Ramrod on the drive is John Chisholm.....The Wrangler is Dakota Smith.....Our Trail Scout is Sean Lone Eagle.....Marianne Robertson is our Head Drover.......But,......most importantly, ...our Trail Cook is Terry Brandon!"

Cheers went up for Terry, as she swept her hat in a low arc, stood in her stirrups and bowed.

"A few more points!" commanded Sam. " Over there are the cattle. They are all Herefords, except for that big old steer..." He pointed. "Over there!...With the long horns!......He's 'Old Bill'. He's been around for a while and knows the trail to Sweet Pasture. He's our lead steer. As you go about chasing strays or just moving the herd and don't know which way to go, just look for Old Bill's long horns and ease the cows toward him."

Sam continued with some trail advice, assignments and safety comments, and concluded by saying. " When we arrive at Sweet Pasture, Terry has planned a special Western barbecue and entertainment from a cowboy singer. We also have a special recognition gift to thank each of you for completing the drive.......Let's have fun!......Any questions?"

There were none.

"If not,......take your positions!" directed Sam.

Sean Lone Eagle moved to the head of the herd with Old Bill. Terry Brandon and Glen O'Rourke dismounted and got into the Ranch truck carrying the food and bedrolls to the lunch stop and then on to the evening camp. The ranch hands had affectionately named the truck, the 'Chuck Truck'.

Emma and Fletcher moved to the rear of the herd in a drag position alongside Marianne.

When everyone was in position, Sam's voice rang out, "Head 'em up!......Move 'em out!"

As he said it, Marianne's bullwhip whistled through the air and snapped a loud "Whhhaack!"

Fletcher, Emma and the other young drovers waived their ropes and yelled, "Yup! Yup!"

The drive was underway!

PART V

The Art of the Scout.

27.

The Scout!

It was a beautiful, sunny morning for the cattle drive. Cattle brayed and leather saddles squeaked as the drive moved out. Old Bill set the pace for a 15-mile day. Lone Eagle rode ahead of the herd scouting for problems. Jose, Fletcher and Nicholas Morgan rode side by side, talking and driving cows. Nicholas was 15 and really enjoyed fishing. The wranglers had put a scabbard on his saddle for his fly fishing rod so that he could fish when they stopped by streams. Barb, Emma, Mitch and Marianne rode together a short distance off.

Jose and Fletcher took particular interest in the way that Lone Eagle on his handsome Paint horse would disappear ghost-like on the right side of the herd almost as they were looking right at him and then reappear like an apparition on the left flank. Jose, Fletcher and Nicholas made a pact to eat lunch with Lone Eagle to learn more about what he was doing, and how he did it—maybe they could even ride with him in the afternoon!

About one o'clock the drive halted in a big meadow filled with violet Asters, Blue Bells and yellow flowered Potentilla. Magpies darted and played tag with each other above the herd while occasional prairie dogs, half hidden in their personal foxholes scolded the invading cattle.

Wendy, Steve, and Debra joined Jose, Fletcher and Nicholas in eating lunch with Lone Eagle. They sat in the shade of a towering 120-foot Ponderosa Pine and looked out over the grazing herd while a light, high country breeze brought mountain scents and refreshing relief from the midday sun.

During initial introductions, they learned that Sean Lone Eagle was a Lakota Sioux who had grown up on the Rosebud Indian Reservation in South Dakota. As a youth, he spent much of his time outdoors with friends under the tutelage of his uncle and grandfather. They passed to Lone Eagle, the traditional skills of horsemanship, tracking, hunting and survival. But in addition, his grandfather taught him secret ways of the scout. While in tribal high school he worked hard to win a scholarship to Caltech where he studied mathematics. He then spent three years as an analyst at an investment bank in New York before returning to Stanford where he had just completed the first year of an MBA. In spite of his time spent in the cities, everyone could see that he loved the out of doors and was at home in it.

Lone Eagle usually went by the name of Sean, but here on the ranch, he preferred Lone Eagle.

As he sipped water and munched on a sandwich, Fletcher asked, "Lone Eagle, what is a scout?"

Lone Eagle hesitated, searching for where to begin, then said. "A scout is much different than many people expect. Most people think of a scout in the sense of the Apache scouts who hunted Geronimo or the Crow scouts who rode with Custer against the Sioux and Cheyenne at the Little Big Horn. These were Indian Army scouts who used their tracking skills to hunt people.......True Indian scouting skills are much greater than this and are used for much different ends.......My grandfather taught me that scouts exist to give life to the people.......Whether it was scouting to find food, water, or shelter,......or protecting the village by scouting ahead of a war party to safely lead them to enemies, the scout used his skills to help his people survive. And his skills went beyond those of an Indian hunter or tracker. The scouts were the 'best of the breed'. As they learned scouting, they were taught to feel the heartbeat of the earth and the 'spirit, which moves through all things."

"What do you mean?" asked Nicholas.

"I understand that you are a good fisherman," said Lone Eagle.

"The best!" proclaimed Nicholas.

"Do you remember when you first started fishing?" asked Lone Eagle.

Nicholas nodded, "Yes!"

Lone Eagle continued, "You would come to a stream, and you would think hard about which bait to use and where to fish? Sometimes it took you 20 minutes to get the bait in the water,......and an hour or more to get a nibble!"

"That's right!" agreed Nicholas.

"And now what happens?" asked Lone Eagle.

"By the time I get to the edge of the stream, I know where I want to fish, and what bait I want to use." replied Nicholas. "I normally get a bite and land a fish within 15 minutes."

"Why is that?" asked Lone Eagle.

"I just know where I would be, and what I would want to eat if I was a fish," said Nicholas.

"In a way with respect to fishing, you have learned to sense and to become part of the 'flow of life.' said Lone Eagle. In the special world of fishing you have learned to feel the temperature, humidity, sunlight, the wind, speed of the water, activity of insects and other factors in the way that the fish senses them. Once you learn to feel the flow of life, you can become part of it,......and in fact by becoming part of it, you become invisible.......By picking the right fly, casting upstream, and making sure that your shadow doesn't fall over the hole, the fish is not aware that you are there. When he senses no danger, the fish is relaxed and is not tentative, or suspicious of your fly when it comes by him,......he strikes!"

"I see what you mean!" said Nicholas.

"But you spoke of the scout in a broader sense," said Jose. "What *does* it mean to be an Indian scout?"

"In my great grandfather's time the scout's *responsibility* was to find shelter, food and water for his people and to protect them. This responsibility heightened the scout's sense of awareness of the world around him. Over time, in many tribes, those who had the gift and accepted the responsibilities of scouting formed secret societies in which they helped each other perfect their skills and select and train new scouts." replied Lone Eagle.

He continued. "Let me help you understand what I mean by 'heightening the sense of awareness of the world around you'"......

"When a hunter tracks a bear, he focuses on following its paw marks in the ground.......*But, beyond that,* a scout studies the paw marks to see how recently the bear has passed and the direction and speed of movement.......*But, beyond that,* the scout knows that by expanding his consciousness and sensing the world around him, he can 'see beyond the mountain'................If he sees deer coming toward him from both sides of a hill, or birds flushing into the air from further down a valley, something is causing that to happen. If the bear has passed recently and no other predators are nearby, it is likely that the bear is scaring the deer or flushing the birds. From this, the scout knows where the bear tracks likely *will be,* and **where the bear is**—not just where the bear was........*But, beyond that,* he studies the tracks to see if the bear is standing or turning to look for something. The scout tries to understand why the bear is moving; to understand '*What motivates the bear?!?*' Is the bear moving to get away from the tracker, or to find berries, honey, grubs, fish, water, another bear or a place to rest?......Knowing the land, the season and the time of day, the scout often knows where the bear can find what it is looking for.......Sensing the rhythm of life in the world around him, and the rhythm of life in the bear being tracked, **the scout often knows where the bear will be**

before the tracks ever get there and sometimes even before the bear knows where it is going . ... This is part of being a scout!"

Lone Eagle smiled and replied thoughtfully, "The scout's art is not just to see what is around him, but to sense the source of tension in the world around him and to learn *why* the tension exists. If animals are running toward him, they are running *from* something even though he cannot see it.......**The scout looks for what is missing** as much as what is present in the rhythm and flow of life. If there are no tracks around a waterhole, there is a reason. He must find it!"

"Lone Eagle," said Wendy. "Does the art of scouting apply to the modern world?"

"Yes." replied Lone Eagle. "The teachings of scouting are as useful today as they were when Pontiac, Cochise and Sitting Bull lived. Reading the rhythm of life in society, the economy or companies is as valuable to us as reading sign in the Appalachian forests was to the Iroquois . ... Most people today do not listen with their ears, *let alone* with their eyes, their experience, their mind or their other senses. People do not look for the pressure points disturbing the rhythm of life, and causing things to happen around them. Their senses are dulled by preoccupation, noise and motion."

He raised his head and looked at the mountain peaks as if seeking a vision. "Here, let me share another thought to help you understand. I read a book, *The Wisdom of the Native Americans* edited by Kent Nerburn, an artist and student of the American Indians. It contained great speeches of Indian Chiefs and leaders. His introduction was so powerfully written, that I memorized some of the words!"..............
Lone Eagle spoke the words:

> Most of us are trained to read with our minds.......We pass over words, compressing them into ideas,...and we use these ideas as the measure of understanding.......But there is another way to read,......where the words themselves take on a life of their own,......and the rhythms and cadences open a floodgate of

images and sympathies, until we feel the heartbeat of their author and sense the lifeblood of the experience that they contain.

It is a way of reading that is more akin to listening to music,...where the sheer power of the sound can move the hearer to tears.

This is the way we should read these great speeches. Like the insistent beat of ceremonial drums, their words weave a hypnotic spell, and the passion of their vision enters the hearts as well as the minds of their listeners.

Lone Eagle continued, "**We need to read companies the way Nerburn encourages us to listen to words.**......Within a company the timing and existence or absence of actions constitute a 'beat of the drums'—the 'rhythm of life'—surrounding that company. If an observer can discipline himself to act like a scout,—by reading the rhythm of life rather than just focusing on following the tracks left by the company's earnings per share (EPS),—it is possible to get into the bear's mind and to anticipate where the 'bear' is going before it knows. **It is the art of 'reading sign' to learn 'what motivates the bear' and to anticipate what he will do next that separates the 'Rich Shareowner' (the scout) from the 'Poor Shareowner' (the tracker) who only sees what has happened.**"

Just as Wendy was about to ask a question, Chisholm announced, "Mount up!"

Lunch was over.

As they cleaned up the lunch area, Wendy, Jose and Fletcher asked Lone Eagle if they could ride with him and learn more about scouting in the afternoon.

Lone Eagle nodded, "Yes."

28.

On The Trail!

"Whhhhaaack!......Whhhhaaack!"

Marianne's bullwhip sounded promptly after Chisholm called for the herd to move out.

Wendy, Fletcher and Jose joined Lone Eagle at the point position and commenced their scouting education. During the early afternoon, Lone Eagle taught them some tracking skills. Fletcher found and followed bear tracks as well as those of antelope and deer. Jose came upon rare, two day old tracks of a cougar, and Wendy discovered a wolf's paw prints. Lone Eagle also showed them how to blend in with the rhythm of the cattle and passing landscape so they became almost invisible—ghost like—to the unconscious observer. Then he showed them how to disappear on one side of the herd and reappear on the other. He pointed out 'pressure points'—where the movement of one thing in nature caused something else to happen. At one point he taught them how to convert a watch to a compass by pointing the short, hour hand in the direction of the sun. When they did that, the direction south was half way between that short hand and the 12 on the watch face.

As the afternoon progressed, Jose and Fletcher became engrossed in locating tracks of different animals. They developed a friendly competition, seeing who could find the most new tracks. They had Lone Eagle confirm the prints before they added them to their list.

Wendy rode beside Lone Eagle.......Gradually their conversation turned to Lone Eagle's three years in New York.

"Lone Eagle," said Wendy, "tell me about your experiences as an investment banking analyst; did your work ever use any of your scouting skills?"

"At first, it didn't!" he replied......."I focused on producing the classic financial analysis expected by investment banks.......But, after three months, I realized that I was merely 'following the bear tracks.' I wasn't explaining what motivated the bear and what he would do next..........I was just doing what everybody else did. I wasn't creating value, and I wasn't having any fun!"

"What did you do?" asked Wendy.

"I called Sam. We had spent several summers together. I trained him in scouting in exchange for lessons in finance!" replied Lone Eagle. "We spoke for an hour, and as usual, Sam asked questions which I should have asked myself. At the end of our talk, I decided that I needed to treat my analytical work on companies like I would treat a scouting mission."

"How so?" quizzed Wendy.

Lone Eagle acknowledged her question, and took several minutes to redirect the herd to a different route by guiding Old Bill. When he returned he said, "I needed to anticipate where the company was going! To do that I needed to identify what 'motivated the bear'- what caused the company to do things?......And, to do that, I needed to learn what drove the culture of the company, and to understand the motivation and character of two key company officers—the Chief Executive Officer (CEO), and the Chief Financial Officer (CFO)."

"Motivation and character of the CEO and CFO?!?" inquired Wendy.

"Yes!" said Lone Eagle, "The CEO and CFO set the culture and direction of the company. If the company is going to change what it is doing or the way it does it, it usually starts with one of them."

"How do you go about discovering culture, motivations and character?" asked Wendy.

He smiled, "Like animals, each company, each person and each set of tracks is similar, yet unique. Some tracks are in the financial statements, the annual report and in the company's mission statement; some are in officers' speeches and the way that they answer questions, or in the content and proactive (or reactive) manner of press releases; some are in news stories; and, many are in the actions of the company and its people in its dealings with employees, suppliers, customers and the community. A scout must treat each track as new, yet related, or he will miss something. And, the scout looks for the company's rhythm of life running through all of them.......But, I have some common approaches which I use in understanding a company and these two key officers."

"Will you share some with me!?" asked Wendy.

"I only share them with fellow scouts!" Lone Eagle deadpanned.

"I'd like to be one!" flirted Wendy.

He chuckled, nodded and began, "My first step is to understand where the company has been and where it might be moving based upon the tracks it's leaving. ......Is it creating Enterprise Value and how?......My second step is to compare the words and actions of company managers to the facts to determine why it's moving the way it's moving .... In this step, I try to determine if the CEO and CFO know that their job is to create Enterprise Value; are they doing it, and can they explain how they are doing it?......The final step is to develop hypotheses and conclusions about where the company is going."

"Elaborate!" Wendy entreated.

Lone Eagle nodded, "The first step—understanding where the company has been—is probably the easiest!......I begin by calculating the company's WACC (Weighted Average Cost of Capital), its Enterprise Value, its market value and its Economic Profit (EP) for the past three years. I also look at what people are paid to do—their incentive plans."

"When calculating the Enterprise Value I force myself to look at the five Value Drivers for the company (sales growth, margin improvement, asset reduction, acquisitions and WACC reduction). But, I particularly focus on the growth rate in Annual Cash Flows, which incorporates the first three Value Drivers. Using a special table that I developed, I compare the growth rate used in calculating Enterprise Value to the growth rate implicit in the market price.......I also attempt to identify material changes in other Value Drivers (such as operating margins, assets, acquisitions or WACC) which account for major differences in the two growth rates."

He continued, "I calculate the current Economic Profit (EP) and its three year trend, to learn if the company is creating or destroying Enterprise Value, i.e. is the company earning its WACC each year? In any single year the EP might be negative—especially if a company is recovering from some set back—but the 3 year trend is an indication of whether there is conscious effort by management to improve EP, or whether the improvement is merely serendipity."

"Another primary track that I look for is the design of the incentive compensation plan. I want to see what management is getting paid to do! Are they being paid to increase Enterprise Value or just accounting EPS?"

Wendy interrupted, "Please go back a step, and tell me a little more about your comment that you developed a table to identify the growth rate implicit in the stock's Market Value."

Lone Eagle retrieved a laminated card from his wallet. "Here is a card showing 'rule of thumb' relationships between P/E's (price to earnings ratios) and growth rates based upon a series of sensitivities done using my basic Enterprise Value model. These growth rates are the growth rate of Annual Cash Flow. The growth rates exclude acquisitions because in most cases the acquisition price usually equals or exceeds the present value of the acquired Enhanced Cash Flow (i.e. Annual Cash Flows including synergies)......Instead of P/E's, it would have been better to use something closer to cash flow ratios such as Price to Earnings Before Interest, Taxes and Amortization (P/EBITA), but while imperfect, P/E's provide a useful 'rule of thumb' because most people have easy access to current P/E's."

Growth Rates Implicit in P/E Ratios

P/E	Implied Annual Growth Rate for 10 Years % p.a.	Size of company sales in 10 years starting from $1mm	Price/Earnings to Growth Rate ('PEG') Ratio
10	0%	$1.0	–
13	5	1.6	2.6
17	10	2.6	1.7
21	15	4.0	1.4
28	20	6.2	1.4
38	25	9.3	1.5
51	30	13.8	1.7
68	35	20.1	1.9
92	40	28.9	2.3
122	45	41.1	2.7
163	50	57.7	3.3

"What are the key assumptions in these numbers, and how do you use them?" asked Wendy.

Lone Eagle responded, "The model assumes a constant growth rate in Annual Cash Flow for 10 years and then no growth thereafter. I stop growth at 10 years because companies usually have to make major investments (i.e. cash flow) to reinvent their products if they are to grow the whole company at high rates beyond 10 years.......**Every company is different! My** *chart works for the vast majority of companies,* **but, you always have to use judgment in the application of any rule of thumb.......**The chart assumes that an equity investor desires to earn 10% p.a. in a tax free account."

"The columns are pretty simple," he continued. "The *first column* shows the price to earnings (P/E) ratio associated with the growth in Annual Cash flows shown in the *second column.* The *third column* is a reality check.......It shows how big the company would be after 10 years, if it grew at the designated growth rate.......For example, if the company's current sales were $1 billion, with a P/E of 92, the implied growth rate of 40% p.a. means that sales would need to be $28.9 billion—excluding acquisitions—in ten years in order to justify the current stock price.......Is that realistic?"

Lone Eagle pointed to the last column. "The *fourth column* shows the Price/Earnings to Growth Ratio. *If* **GAAP earnings were a good proxy for cash flow, then this column reflects the maximum ratio of P/E to Growth Rate that would still yield the Shareowner a 10% return.** Since GAAP earnings are a weak proxy for cash flow, a number of investors say that they will only invest in a stock whose PEG ratio is less than 1.0."

"Say that again!" said Wendy.

"Sure," he replied. "First, recall that earlier this week, Georgia and Steve pointed out that Cash Flow was 2 ½ times more highly correlated with stock price than EPS?"

"Yes?!?" responded Wendy.

"Well, what happens if a Shareowner can't easily get the data to calculate cash flow and Economic Profit, and therefore, is forced to use GAAP earnings?......*Also*, what does a prudent investor do if he has to use a growth rate that is just his best guesstimate of the company's growth rate over the next ten years?"

"He builds in a safety margin!" answered Wendy.

"Right!" said Lone Eagle. "And, **many investors have said that buying a stock with a PEG ratio of 1.0 or less gives them a sufficient safety margin to cover these two key assumptions.**"

"Wow!" exclaimed Wendy. "**This has a major impact on the efficiency of the stock market! The less comfortable people are with the information about a stock, the lower the price that they will pay for it!**"

"That's the reality of it," said Lone Eagle. "May I finish up one other point on my chart?"

"Absolutely!" nodded Wendy.

Lone Eagle continued. "Assuming that one time events are not distorting earnings or stock price, comparing the implied growth rate to the historic growth rate tells me a lot. For example, if a company has a 60% market share in a market growing 10% per year, an implied P/E growth rate of 25% is unrealistic. The company would have 100% market share and outgrow the market in five years!......It is unrealistic to assume that their competition will abandon the market—especially if margins and growth are high! Therefore, with *extremely high* probability, the company's stock is overvalued."

Lone Eagle looked at Wendy, "Also, if nothing has changed, and the growth rate implied by a company's P/E is materially above its historic growth rate, it is likely that the stock is being traded by momentum investors and is not trading based upon its Enterprise Value."

"What's wrong with a stock trading based on its stock price momentum?" questioned Wendy.

"Nothing!" replied Lone Eagle....."So long as the investor recognizes that's how it's trading, *and* recognizes how vulnerable the price is!..........**Sam and I have a name for investing in stocks which trade at the excessively high growth rates implied by these high P/E's.**"

"What's that?" asked Wendy.

"**The 'Greater Fool Theory of Investing'**!" replied Lone Eagle

Wendy laughed, "Why's that?"

"**When growth rates implied by the P/E are unrealistically high, the only way for a Shareowner to realize value is to find a 'greater fool' to buy the stock at an even higher P/E** (and, therefore, a higher implied growth rate—or lower return). **Absent that greater fool, eventually the stock price will fall—or regress—to the Enterprise Value.......That can be a long fall for a 100 P/E stock!**"

"Makes sense!" laughed Wendy........"Leave it to you and Sam to give it such a politically correct name!"

Lone Eagle laughed as he spurred his horse and loped toward Jose.

Growth Rates of Annual Cash Flow Implicit in P/E Ratios

P/E	Implied Annual Growth Rate for 10 Years % p.a.	Size of company sales in 10 years starting from $1mm	Price/Earnings to Growth Rate ('PEG') Ratio
10	0%	$1.0	-
13	5	1.6	2.6
17	10	2.6	1.7
21	15	4.0	1.4
28	20	6.2	1.4
38	25	9.3	1.5
51	30	13.8	1.7
68	35	20.1	1.9
92	40	28.9	2.3
122	45	41.1	2.7
163	50	57.7	3.3

This model assumes a constant growth rate of Annual Cash Flow for ten years,
and no growth thereafter.
This is reasonable because most companies will need major capital or research investment by the tenth year in order to extend the growth curve.

The first column is the P/E (price to earnings) ratio.

The second column shows the implied growth rate of Annual Cash Flow associated with a given P/E if the Shareowner is to earn 10% in a tax free account.

Column three is a reality check!
It shows in dollar terms how big the company's sales would be at the end of 10 years if it grew at the implied annual growth rate.

Column four is the 'PEG' ratio. It shows the maximum Price to Earnings ratio that a Shareowner would pay for the growth in the second column if he wanted to earn 10%.

Because of inefficiencies in projecting future growth and in the correlation of GAAP earnings to cash flow,
many investors limit their purchases to stocks with a PEG ratio of 1 or less.

29.

Moving On!

Lone Eagle had been gone about 45 minutes. During that time, some of the cattle on the lead flanks had been drifting away from the herd, and Wendy drove them back in. She saw Fletcher and Jose signal Lone Eagle, and he rode over to join them. It looked like they got off their horses to study some animal tracks, and then they mounted and appeared to follow the tracks. They slowly rode up and over the ridgeline to the southwest of the herd. While he was gone, Wendy had time to absorb some of the ideas they had discussed.

The shadows in the valley were getting longer, indicating late afternoon when Lone Eagle trotted up and slowed to a walk beside her. He spoke first, "Fletcher found that cougar's tracks again. Pretty fresh! Wouldn't expect to see them this time of day or so close to the herd. We followed them back up over the ridge. He's moving away from the herd. Looks like he may have just been passing through. I don't expect that he'll trouble us with all the game food that's around this time of year."

Wendy felt comforted by his assurances and presence. Seeing a mountain lion in a zoo was one thing; the thought of encountering one in the wilds of the San Juan Mountains was another! She didn't reveal her concern as she said, "For the sake of the calves, I'm glad he's gone!"

Lone Eagle nodded and hid a smile.

She continued, "I'd like to pick up the conversation we were having before you educated me about the 'Greater Fool Theory of Investing!'"

They both chuckled.

"What other tracks do you look for in order to determine where a company has been and where it's going?" she asked.

Lone Eagle nudged a cow back toward the herd, then responded, "Just like rain is the life blood of a ranch, cash flow is the life blood of a company. A company can survive for years without earnings.......It can't survive a month without cash! I study the cash flow statement to see where management is getting cash and where they are using it—just like a doctor studies a blood analysis. In doing this I discover many tracks and pressure points not apparent from the income statement. For example, management may be reporting increasing GAAP (Generally Accepted Accounting Principles) income. However, studying the cash flow in conjunction with the income statement and annual report, I can learn if the income is coming from improved business performance, from changes in accounting rules or from management's proactive 'gaming' of the income statement. As you know, there are a large number of actions that create GAAP income, but not cash. They range from changes in the actuarial assumptions on employee benefit plans to reducing depreciation expense by lengthening depreciation periods on capital assets. The changes may be more esoteric such as divestitures which create one time GAAP earnings gains, but which reduce Enterprise Value because the after tax proceeds can't be reinvested at a high enough return to equal the present value of the cash flows of the asset sold."

Lone Eagle looked at Wendy, "The reason that cash flow is more reliable than the income statement is that cash has to reconcile to real payments made to third parties and to the bank accounts—real cash with third parties! Accounting numbers don't! Accounting statements, such as the income statement, only have to reconcile with other company accounting statements prepared by management using their own discretion in applying constantly changing GAAP accounting rules to the company.......I look hard for anomalies between the cash flow, income statement and balance sheet, and try to identify the reason why.......One thing I notice is that managements who are having difficulty creating Enterprise Value, rely heavily on accounting changes, one time charge-offs, asset sales, divestitures and acquisitions to attempt to hide their difficulty in creating Enterprise Value (net present value of cash flow) by managing the core business."

"You used the term 'gaming'. What did you mean?" asked Wendy.

Lone Eagle responded, "In this context, 'gaming' means knowingly taking action to achieve accounting results, such as increasing current GAAP income, even though the actions destroy Enterprise Value."

"Give me an example," said Wendy.

He answered, "A prime example would be the use of 'financial engineering' techniques such as the sale of receivables to get assets off the balance sheet. Management's rationale might be to improve the accounting ratio, Return on Capital Employed (ROCE), by reducing capital reported on the GAAP balance sheet (i.e. to 'dress the balance sheet'). The problem is that the financing cost charged by the banks on the sale of the receivables has a higher cash cost than financing the receivables with debt on the balance sheet.......Even though this technique improves the accounting ROCE ratio, the real impact of the higher cash cost is to destroy Enterprise Value!"

He continued, "In this case, the 'gaming' becomes a naive form of deception on the part of management. Naive because knowledgeable Shareowners (and the debt rating agencies) understand that the discounted receivables are still being used in the business, and knowledgeable investors/creditors will add them back when computing Economic Profit, Enterprise Value and debt capacity. The Shareowners will see that the result of management's action was to knowingly destroy

Enterprise Value by trading cash flow for reduced debt on the GAAP balance sheet." said Lone Eagle.

"What else do you look for to determine what 'motivates the bear'?" she asked.

"There are many other things," he replied, "I'll mention a few important ones. For each of them I try to understand if the action is taken to consciously create Enterprise Value (net present value of cash flow), or whether Enterprise Value is merely a by-product. If management destroys cash flow merely to achieve accounting ends, it's a red flag! When I see it, I dig deeper to find out if management is simply unaware that its actions are costing cash, or even worse, is management intentionally trading cash and, therefore, Enterprise Value for accounting results on which their personal bonus is paid?!"

- Business Model—I try to understand if the business model makes sense and produces Enterprise Value. Most dot com business models were defective because they did not have a rational way to create Annual Cash Flow, therefore, Enterprise Value.

- Business Vision and Strategy—Does management have a vision for what business the company should be in, and does it have a strategy for implementing the Business Model(s) which produces Enterprise Value?

- Goal Pyramid—Where does creation of Enterprise Value rank in the goal hierarchy?

- Does the company have a renewal/reinvention process to remain competitive and to create increasing Enterprise Value? This is especially important the bigger the company gets.

- Financial Goals—Is the financial goal directed to increasing Enterprise Value? Is it simple to understand and implement on a day-to-day basis?

- Incentive Plans—Are incentive plans directly tied to creation of Enterprise Value (e.g. increasing the $ Economic Profit each year)?
- Are business and financial risks in balance?

"That's a new one! What do you mean by balancing business and financial risks?" asked Wendy.

Lone Eagle jumped from his horse, grabbed a stick and sketched out a picture in the dirt as he spoke, "My ancestors knew the importance of living in harmony with the world around them……They knew that corn wouldn't grow in winter; therefore, they had to store food or starve. They knew that when things get out of balance, nature acts to restore that balance……If a deer population breeds too heavily for the land to support it with food, the weaker animals die, thus, allowing the rest of the herd to survive and to grow stronger."

As he pointed to the rough sketch in the dirt, he said, "If I could draw better, there would be a blindfolded Goddess of Justice in a long, white, Roman robe standing behind my scales to emphasize that nature and competition are great, impartial equalizers. Let me give two illustrations of how harmony applies to the business of creating Enterprise Value……….The first example relates to companies who have high business risk—such as when introducing new or major products. These companies sometimes make the mistake of simultaneously increasing their financial risk. This happens when they take on too much debt, and, therefore, reduces their ability to survive business risks such as cost over runs or longer than anticipated product introduction cycles……I recall at least one dot com which used cash to repurchase stock while it was still loosing money, and before it had even developed its product! It ran out of cash and had to declare bankruptcy……….The second illustration is merely the observation that the market value of a stock regresses over time to its Enterprise Value;……the act of regressing is merely an act of restoring balance or harmony!"

Lone Eagle's Scales
'Balance Breeds Harmony'

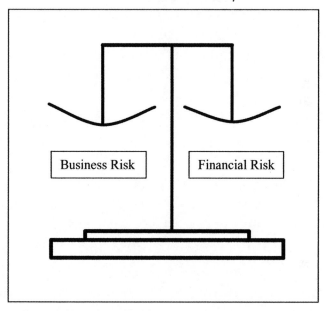

Wendy saw him frown when he said, "Even when a company's actions are intended to create Enterprise Value, justice comes quickly if the management team doesn't retain balance and perspective in their actions. The speed of competition is too swift to let imbalances survive; the imbalances become someone else's opportunity."

Lone Eagle chuckled as he looked up at her and said, "Anyone who has spent time on a horse knows the sudden, hard justice that comes from loosing balance!"

She laughed with him.

As he mounted, Wendy asked, "So, how do all these things like WACC, Enterprise Value, Economic Profit and Goal Pyramids help you to get inside the head of the bear and understand the motivation and character of the CEO and CFO?"

"Recall that I first look at a company to determine if and how the company is creating Enterprise Value.......My second step is to determine if the CEO and CFO consciously know and are proactively doing their primary job of creating Enterprise Value."

"Let me share with you some of the most basic questions which I use to determine if the CEO and CFO know that their job is to create Enterprise Value:

- Do the CEO and CFO know the company's WACC? ......

  If they don't know the WACC, they can't manage *to* it!......If they won't tell Shareowners the WACC, they are hiding something. They could be hiding that they don't understand it, *or* they may not want to be held accountable to it. In any case, the Shareowners have a problem!

- Do the CEO and CFO understand what WACC represents?

  If they do not understand that the WACC represents the minimum return that the company needs to generate on the *entire* business just to maintain the current stock price, then they cannot be consciously managing Enterprise Value or its proxy, Economic Profit.

- Do the CEO and CFO know the company's Enterprise Value and what it represents (net present value of cash flow)?

  If they can't *define* Enterprise Value, then they can't be consciously working to increase it.......The CEO & CFO must be able and willing to explain the difference between the company's market value and Enterprise Value—even if it is just to say that there is a temporary supply/demand imbalance!

- Do the CEO and CFO know the company's Economic Profit (EP) for the past three years?

Do they know the company's EP and the concepts behind EP?......Do they understand its relationship to Enterprise Value?......

(Enterprise Value = present value of EP + beginning capital)?......

Can they explain trends in EP?......Can they explain the source of future growth in $ EP?

- Have the CEO & CFO established and communicated the company's Goal Pyramid?

    Does it include increasing Enterprise Value? If Enterprise Value isn't the first goal, how are conflicts between goals resolved?

- What are the management incentive plans?

    Are incentive plans focused on increasing Enterprise Value? ......Are they based upon a simple proxy for increasing Enterprise Value such as Economic Profit (EP)?"

"This is fascinating," said Wendy........"But, you said that your questions told you something of the character and motivation of the CEO and CFO. What did you mean?"

Lone Eagle rode silently for a minute, and then slowly looked to the sky........"My grandfather taught me that when you first meet a man, you must study his tracks and listen to his words.......If they are the same, then tomorrow you only need listen to his words........If they are different, then tomorrow you must only believe his tracks!"

They rode in silence for the next half hour.......They each knew the truth in the Grandfather's words and how the words related to top managers.

Finally, as they pulled into view of the evening camp, Wendy asked, "Why did you leave the analyst position at the investment bank?"

"I felt that I was misleading people." replied Lone Eagle.

"What do you mean by that?!?" she gently challenged.

He said, "The CEO's, CFO's and investing public, who seek advice from investment bankers, analysts, or brokers expect that we are representing their interests.......It is impossible!......No matter how hard an individual tries, he is always influenced by how he is measured by the person who writes his paycheck........In the press of business today, most people forget that most brokerage and investment banking incentives are paid on the fees earned from selling stock or closing a deal this year.......The tracks evidence that the customer is this year's transaction. Next year takes care of itself.......If my grandfather had known Latin, I think that he would have reminded us 'Caveat Emptor'.......'Let the buyer beware.'"

They smiled a frustrated smile at each other and rode toward camp.

Balance Breeds Harmony!

Lone Eagle's Scales

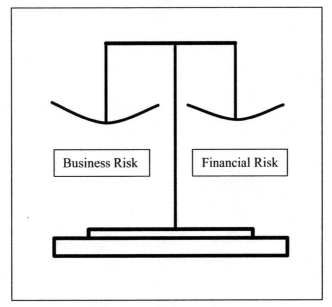

On Character:

"When you first meet a man
you must study his tracks and listen to his words…..
If they are the same, then tomorrow you only need listen to his
words….
If they are different, then tomorrow you must only believe his
tracks!"

Lone Eagle

PART VI

Riding for the Brand!

30.

People Do what you Pay them To Do!.......
But, a Job isn't a Lottery Ticket!

By 8:00, Wednesday evening the setting sun had painted the high clouds a deep, florescent, reddish orange against a fading, crystal blue sky. It looked like a Terry Redlin landscape. Twenty minutes earlier a few clouds low in the west had been framed in brilliant gold. Wendy thought to herself that the sunsets in the high Rockies were magnificent!

The camp had two fires. The smaller fire had been used to cook dinner, and the larger fire had been built about 30 feet away to let people warm themselves as the high country chill set in for the night. The wranglers and guests had just finished dinner consisting of green salad, barbecued pork and chicken, corn on the cob, baked potatoes and broccoli. For dessert they had warm apple cobbler with plenty of caramel sauce and a touch of thick cream. Coffee, hot chocolate and warm, oatmeal raisin cookies were plentiful.......This dude dinner was a far cry from the beans, salt pork, cornmeal, molasses and coffee consumed on the old cattle drives!

Most of the campers gathered around the large fire where some of the wranglers and guests got out the guitars and harmonicas packed on the Chuck Truck. Soon, they had a good old-fashioned cowboy sing-along and western tall tale fest going. Sam, Mitch, Wendy, Barb and others in Sam's Coffee Club, as they had come to be known, grabbed their saddles and wondered over to the smaller fire. Sam threw a few more logs on to the fire for heat and light, while everyone arranged their saddles around the fire as back rests.

With coffee in hand, the fire's warming ambiance, and a beautiful San Juan mountain sunset in front of them, Sam's group leaned back against their saddles and talked. The occasional breath of pungent wood smoke added flavor to their coffee, tears to their eyes and life to the conversation.

After 15 minutes, Mitch stiffly repositioned himself and with a grimace said. "Sam, it was a long ride up here for some of us...... (There were a few laughs at Mitch's expense at that statement!)......But, it was worth it! This is an experience and scene that we will remember for a lifetime!"

There were many concurring nods.

Mitch continued, "Sam, if it's OK with the group, I'd like to return to a topic that Jose raised yesterday morning. We were talking about what caused value to happen, and we were skirting the issue of incentive plans when Jose said that we should pay people for creating Enterprise Value, but stop paying them with stock options. I'd like to explore that further."

The group seemed willing, so Sam said, "Sure! Perhaps we should let Jose pick up where he left off."

Jose sat up straighter and fumbled with his saddle, "I'll do the best that I can after a full day and on a full stomach!"

There were a number of sympathizers in the audience!

He found his saddlebags and put them on his lap. "With your permission, Ladies and Gentlemen, let me repeat what I said yesterday. I said that we should stop using stock options as a *primary incentive*. My reason is that that we are running a business, not a lottery!.......A job is not a lottery ticket!"

Jose picked up a stick and scratched on the ground an abbreviated version of Debra's chalkboard sketch."

$$\text{S/O Val} \quad = \quad \text{E. V.} \quad + \quad (\, \text{S \& D} \,)$$

"Recall that earlier this week, Debra wrote the factors which created Shareowner Value on the chalkboard. We said that creation (or destruction) of Shareowner Value is determined by two factors: Enterprise Value (the net present value of cash flow), and supply and demand for the company's stock.

In their mind's eye, people recalled Debra's Chalkboard Sketch:

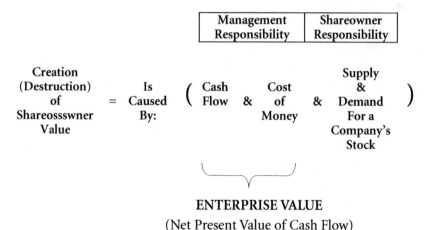

ENTERPRISE VALUE
(Net Present Value of Cash Flow)

He pointed to the letters 'EV' sketched on the ground in the firelight. "As a Shareowner, I should be paying managers to improve what they control. *Managers control Enterprise Value,* and therefore, incentive plans should reward them competitively based upon how much

Enterprise Value they create.......*Managers do not control the supply & demand for a company's stock,* and therefore, they should be neither penalized nor rewarded for market serendipity."

Jose looked his audience in the eye, and became more animated. "There is no reason to pay CEO's or CFO's incentives of $5mm, $10mm, $20mm, $100mm or more a year when they don't produce many hundreds of multiples of that in Enterprise Value. CEO's and CFO's are bright people, but they are not unique.......Let me use a sports analogy......There are good players; there are team franchise players, and there are game franchise players. Michael Jordan and Arnold Palmer are examples of game franchise players. Bill Gates, Jack Welch and Lee Iacocca might fall into the game or the team franchise category. The rest are good players, but their performance does not justify the pay of a Gates, Welch, Iacocca, Jordan or Palmer.........**We must get away from the idea that the CEO/CFO and other senior jobs are entitlements to lottery winnings!......CEO's and CFO's are paid to do a job just like any other hired hand. They are paid to create Enterprise Value.** If their performance and competitive conditions justify a $5mm plus payday, then let's make sure it is paid—*if and when* they lead creation of a proportionate amount of Enterprise Value. Incentives should not be paid merely because the company's stock sector is in favor and increases the value of stock options!.......**It is the Shareowners, not the CEO's and CFO's who are taking the capital risks of the business! They should get the rewards!**"

With larceny in his eye, Mitch said, "I take it that you feel strongly about this?"

Without missing a beat, Jose grinned and responded, "Only when it applies to others!"

Everyone laughed.

Mitch then asked, "Jose, what do you think is a fair incentive for a CEO?"

"There is no one right answer," replied Jose. "As a Shareowner, I think that it is fair to suggest that the incentive pool paid to the entire management team should be about 25% of the incremental Economic Profit created each year—of course it would be put into a three year pool so that it stays at risk.......Let me give an example. If last year's EP was $5mm, and this year's is $15mm, then the bonus pool would be 25% of the $10mm ($15mm—$5mm) increase or $2.5mm."

Jose continued, "Since the CEO and CFO are part of a large team, I don't think that any one person should get more than 10% of the pool.......Note, that if the CEO or CFO are Shareowners in their own right, they deserve to get the same appreciation as other Shareowners."

At this point, Jose paused, reached into his saddlebags and pulled out some papers. "Recall that yesterday morning, when we were talking about lessons learned from the Old Trail Bosses, Barb asked me to explain what caused value to happen.......We were interrupted by the day's activities, but knowing Barb to be the tenacious CEO that she is,......I had the ranch office make up these laminates to make our continuing discussion easier."

Jose then passed out the laminates and people studied them in the fading twilight......."People do what you pay them to do!......So, before designing incentive plans, we need to understand how incentive plans create Enterprise Value and fit into something which I call the 'Value Circle.'"

Jose put his card on the ground and lit it up with a flashlight.

He commented. "Look at the side of the card labeled 'Value Circle'. **This Value Circle shows the four critical things a company must do to cause creation of Enterprise Value.** *When all four happen together, they will create a renewal culture that will keep the company changing and adapting in order to continually create Enterprise Value.* If a company doesn't complete the first three elements of the Value Circle before designing the incentive plans, the incentive plans will be sub-optimal at best, and at their worst, will proactively cause destruction of Enterprise Value.......Let me explain."

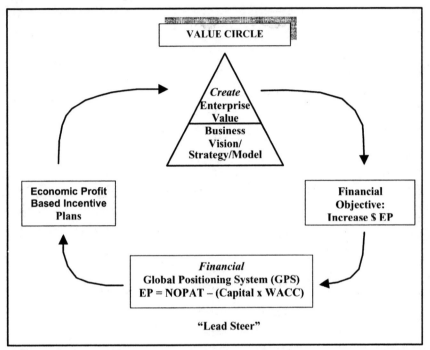

Jose pointed to the triangle at the top of the circle. "As we discussed yesterday morning, the first step for a company is to know what it is trying to do—'what it is about.' To do this, the company must reassess its goal pyramid and make creation of Enterprise Value its primary goal."

Jose then pointed to the bottom box. "To create Enterprise Value, we need to give people doing the work, a simple technique to use in thinking about their day to day decisions in a way which creates Enterprise Value. *My company uses Economic Profit (or EP), as our Lead Steer* for three reasons:

- *First, it is easy for people to use.* It tells people if their decision is creating or destroying Economic Profit —my proxy for Enterprise Value, and gives them a *real time* "rule of thumb' for the tradeoff between using a dollar of capital versus a dollar of operating expense to solve a problem;

- *Second, EP is mathematically related to Enterprise Value.* **This relationship is a mathematical certainty, not merely correlation.** The Enterprise Value is equal to the present value of EP discounted at WACC (Weighted Average Cost of Capital) plus the beginning capital;

- *Finally, EP is easy to use in incentive plans.* This is critical to closing the Value Circle as we will discuss in a minute."

He then pointed to the far right box titled 'Financial Objective', and said, "A company needs to identify and communicate a financial goal which not only creates Enterprise Value each year, but which creates the 'right' amount of Enterprise Value each year. At my company *we currently target a 50% increase in $ Economic Profit each year.* We then agree on a target dollar EP with each profit and cost center. The individual targets add up to the total corporate goal."

Jose then said, " *Now we get to the left box labeled 'Economic Profit Based Incentive Plans'.* Before we talk about the structure of incentive plans, let's turn to the back of the laminate and talk about why they exist."

> The Objective of Incentive Plans
> is to:
>
> 1. Direct
>
> 2. Motivate
>
> 3. Attract
>
> 4. Retain
>
> People in the creation of Enterprise Value!

"Obviously, we have incentive plans to attract and retain people. These aspects principally relate to the upper limit and expected size of the incentive pay out. These are the easiest, most obvious and most worked of the four reasons for incentive plans. They are also the least important. **A company can attract and retain the best people in the world, but if they aren't doing the right things, the creative people can actually be proactively destroying Enterprise Value** "

Jose continued, "*The real challenge is to design incentive plans which direct and motivate people to do the right things.* To do that, the entire Value Circle must be in place. *The incentive plan is the last step to be completed*, and it *is a derivative of the other three steps.*"

Steve interjected, "Jose, I like your Value Circle! It's what the lawyers would call an elegant model—simple, yet comprehensive! It really does highlight the need to integrate the right goals with simple financial models and incentive plans in order to motivate and cause the right action."

Barb then asked, "Jose, what are some of the biggest mistakes which you have seen in incentive plan design?"

"There are five design mistakes which have severely hurt Shareowners," replied Jose.

- *The first mistake was incenting people to increase Earnings Per Share (EPS).* This has had many bad consequences:

    1)   People did the easy thing; they became better at managing accounting rules to increase EPS than at managing the business to create Enterprise Value. It has been estimated that approximately 50% of the increase in EPS of the S&P 500 stocks in the 1990's resulted from changes in accounting rules or management discretion in applying the rules;

    2)   People actually destroyed Enterprise Value in the process of managing EPS. To increase EPS, they would cut investment, research or sales staff which reduced future Economic Profit;

    3)   Managers used acquisitions to buy sales and earnings. However, by paying more than the Enhanced Cash Flow of the acquired company, they actually destroyed Enterprise Value of the acquirer.

- *The second mistake was in granting stock options to too many people.* There have been two primary problems with this:

    1)   People who had incentive stock options were rewarded simply because company stock quadrupled as the US stock market increased by 300% during the '90's, even though they created no Enterprise Value in the company.

    2)   People with large gains on their incentive stock options required even greater incentives to do the same job—even though they were not creating proportionate increases in Enterprise Value.

- *The third mistake was in treating incentive compensation payouts as if they were lotteries* or a gold rush. Just to fill jobs, Boards were paying mediocre managers as if they were super stars.

- *The fourth mistake was that Boards were not defining growth correctly.* They defined growth in terms of EPS, or sales, or net income. **Very few defined growth as growth in Enterprise Value or its proxy, Economic Profit.**

- *Finally, many companies set payouts based on performance at the corporate level.* Many times executive decisions such as one time charge-offs or acquisitions would knock employees out of incentives which they had worked hard all year to achieve—a very demoralizing situation. To get the most out of the incentive plans, the payout should be based as closely as possible on the performance of an individual's work group.

After Jose concluded, Ed Rogers spoke up in an unusually humble and reflective voice. "I think it's true that people do what you pay them to do!......I think it's also fair to say that equity analysts as well as Shareowners and Boards have been encouraging managers to manage EPS rather than Enterprise Value. **Unfortunately, it is becoming clear that we encouraged and paid people to do the wrong thing; we encouraged and paid them to arbitrage the accounting rules to create EPS rather than to create Enterprise Value!**......We are all now paying for that mistake!"

Steve nodded agreement, **"Anybody can cut costs and play accounting games. There is no genius in that! The genius is in the ability to lead and motivate people to grow Enterprise Value!"**

Barb spoke up, "Jose, in listening to your comments, I see that my company has made some important mistakes. Perhaps if I share some of them, they will be helpful to others in understanding how the mistakes hurt us.......We have three plans:

- A one year plan based upon growth in sales and net income;

- A three year plan based upon growth in EPS (earnings per share); and
- A 10 year stock option plan based upon stock price growth!"

"As I reflect on discussions this week, I see how these plans are in conflict with each other and with creation of Enterprise Value. For example:

- An acquisition will increase sales, net income and EPS, but if it costs more than the Enhanced Cash Flow, it will decrease Enterprise Value and eventually reduce stock price as it regresses to the new Enterprise Value;
- A share repurchase may increase EPS in the three-year plan, but the interest expense decreases net income in the one-year plan. If the repurchase is done at a price above Enterprise Value per Share, it will actually destroy Enterprise Value, therefore stock price in the longer run;
- There is a lot of room for legitimate confusion as well as gaming. For example, sales and net income can be increased by offering customers lower prices and extended credit terms. The result may be to reduce Enterprise Value due to lower sales margins and increased capital invested in receivables.
- And, worst of all, none of the three incentives will with certainty increase Enterprise Value."

Now, Mitch asked, "Jose, how would you structure an incentive plan?"

Jose nodded, acknowledging the question. "Let me give you a template which can be refined for specific companies. The design uses EP as the Lead Steer because it is mathematically related to Enterprise Value. But to ensure that people don't do things in the current year that hurt the future, we create a separate individual pool for each individual's incentives over several years. The objective of the plan is to keep it simple and to ensure that it causes the company's $ EP to increase each

year. There are two plans both focused on dollars of Economic Profit. I have added a third plan that helps focus and incent managers by having them invest their own money.

1.   *Plan 1: A one year plan based upon $ increase in EP.* Most people would be in this plan which is based upon the **increase in $ EP at the business unit level.** For more senior people, larger portions would be based upon increase in $ EP at the company level. There might be derivative goals related to effectiveness or efficiency in cost or administrative centers, but **the objective is to keep the design simple and as close as possible to the $ EP formula.** The more that **derivative goals are** used, the more that judgments of plan administrators are substituted for judgments of the people on the front lines who are closest to the marketplace. This substitution is **very dangerous in a dynamic environment.......Each year the bonus would be put into the employee's personal pool and 1/3 of the pool would be paid to the employee.** This way, people are deterred from making short-term decisions that reduce long-term creation of EP, and, therefore, Enterprise Value.

2.   *Plan 2: If necessary for competitive reasons, a three-year plan could be established for senior people.* The plan could be based upon cumulative increase in the company's $ EP over the 3 years. It could be paid out 50% in cash and 50% in stock options. Some other appropriate mix could be selected. The options would be exercisable at any time within 10 years. The options have an initial value equal to the cash bonus, but they would not be 'in the money'. The exercise price would be the current stock price on the date of grant.........Although, I could be persuaded that the strike price should be the

Enterprise Value at the end of the year prior to grant IF, the options were not exercisable for five years under any circumstances (other than sale of the company)—including departure of the grant recipient.

3. *Plan 3: Stock ownership.* While not a plan per se, the company would have a stock ownership requirement so that managers understand what risk and reward means to the Shareowner. All managers would have to own stock in the company equal to one times annual compensation. Officers would have to own two times compensation, The Chairman, CEO, COO, and CFO would have to own three times annual compensation, and the Board members would each have to own at least the dollar equivalent of the average officer. Ownership in employee 401k and similar benefit plans counts toward the requirement!"

Mitch said, "Earlier this week you said not to pay people with stock options, yet now you have them in the mix. Can you reconcile that?"

"Yes." replied Jose. **"The stock options are earned only if (1) necessary to be competitive for talent, and (2) *after* the employee has created Enterprise Value.** The options are not 'in the money' on the grant date. They only have value if the stock price increases above the price on the grant date during the time after the grant date. There would be no $100mm paydays for CEO's unless on their watch, they created at least $50 billion of Enterprise Value (or some similar competitive ratio), *and* the stock price increased."

Mitch commented, "While no plans are perfect, I like your approach. I think that it's comprehensive! As you said, we often forget, especially in the case of compensation of top officers, that we are trying to create an incentive plan, not sure fire lottery winners!"

"I agree," said Barb. "We are going to have to make changes in the Value Circle at our company!"

Sam offered final remarks on incentive plans. "Let me make another point about stock options.....Recall that on Tuesday morning, Steve told us that a company's Enterprise Value increases 11.5% when the WACC declines 1%. Also recall that I said that arbitrageurs affect the supply & demand for a stock in the short run. The arbitrageurs affect the stock price by buying or selling on interest rate movements initiated by the Fed. So, mathematically, **a tax free arbitrageur would move the stock price up 11.5% every time that borrowing costs declined 1%.......Management had nothing to do with this; yet, the value of their stock options just increased by the amount of the 11.5% increase in stock price! That's a pretty big move either for or against management which is caused by serendipity!**"

Sam concluded, "For the Shareowner, alchemy doesn't exist. People do what you pay them to do. If you pay them to do nothing, they will do it and make themselves look busy doing it.......No matter how good the incentive plan design, it is important to 'Keep it simple!' and to compliment it with good leadership!"

People do what you pay them to do!
be sure that you tell them....
what you want them to do!

The real challenge is to design incentive plans that direct and motivate people
to do the right things!

This Value Circle shows the four critical things a company must do
to cause creation of Enterprise Value.
When all four happen together,
they will create a renewal culture
which will keep the company changing
to continually create Enterprise Value!

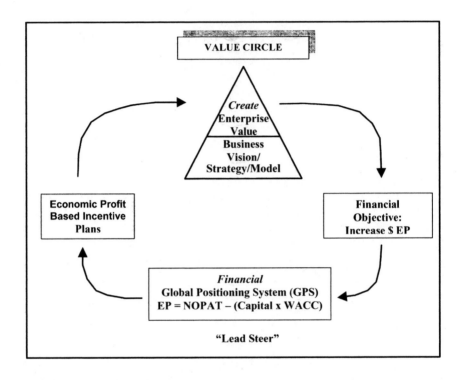

Incentive Plans are not Lotteries!

31.

In Cash We Trust!

Debra had listened intently to the discussion on compensation. As the discussion concluded, she turned to Sam and said, "I've noticed that whenever Economic Profit or Enterprise Value comes up, whether the topic is goal setting, compensation or something else, we always have to modify the accounting statements to come up with a measure of Enterprise Value. I once thought that the income statement was supposed to tell the Shareowner how the company was doing, and whether the company was creating value. *It clearly doesn't*! In fact in many cases the income statement tells you the opposite of what an Economic Profit or detailed Enterprise Value calculation reveals.......Why is that? Where did the accountant's go wrong?"

"She's right!" said Tom, "It seems that, as Shareowners, we are saying, 'In Cash We Trust', but the public financials make it difficult to find the information we need, and they certainly don't provide meaningful measures of value creation!"

As a sharp wisp of wind blew sparks from the fire, Nancy shivered and snuggled closer to Steve. Sam gingerly placed two logs on the fire and looked at Debra and Tom with an empathetic smile......."Somewhere I read that at any point in history, the sophistication of accounting is a reflection of the level of civilization........It seems to me that either society hasn't come very far in the past 2,000 years, or accounting is about to take a quantum leap forward to catch up to civilization."

Steve laughed and spoke loudly with humor. "Are there any accountants in the crowd who care to rebut that?"

Everyone laughed, and Sam laughed loudest.......principally at himself!

"I have been known to overstate my case a time or two,......but, only to make a point!" he chuckled.......Then he turned more serious......."This isn't one of those times!......If you think about it, the current structure of financial statements is designed to give information to asset-based lenders[8], and it is evolving to provide more information to cash flow based lenders[9]. Yet, in spite of the advances in capital market theory and in the Shareowner's need to know valuation data, accountants have not stepped up to the plate by creating a GAAP Valuation Statement designed to give Shareowners easy access to basic valuation information."

"Why don't they?" quizzed Tom.

As Sam took a swig of coffee, Steve jumped in, "I could speculate on a number of things such as the fact that accountants might jeopardize their audit fees by coming into conflict over valuations with management. The conflict would result from the fact that in today's market, most companies aren't earning their WACC (Weighted Average Cost of Capital); in fact most companies are overvalued when their market value is compared to any reasonable estimate of Enterprise Value."

"Steve, how can you say that!!?" challenged Debra.

---

8. Asset-Based Lenders: Lenders who want to ensure that asset values exceed loan value by a comfortable safety margin.

9. Cash Flow Based Lenders: Lenders who want to ensure that the business is generating sufficient cash flow to service the principal and interest on the debt with a comfortable safety margin.

"This week, some of us have seen a table which Lone Eagle put together showing a 'rule of thumb' relationship between price to earnings (P/E) ratios and the related growth rates needed to produce a 10% return to Shareowners. That chart indicated that a P/E of 17 means that a company has to grow 10% p.a. to produce a 10% return for Shareowners (8% above an inflation rate of 2%).......Think about that in the context of the economy and the S&P 500.......If the S&P 500 has a P/E ratio of 28—implying a 20% annual 10-year growth rate for all the S&P 500 companies—do you think that the S&P 500—therefore, the companies in it—are over or under valued?......The real economy is only growing about 2%!"

The group contemplated in a stunned silence.....It was as if their collective jaws had dropped!

After a minute, Sam restarted the conversation; "**The accounting profession needs to reflect on the fact that if they don't develop a GAAP Valuation Statement, they have something at risk even greater than fees.**"

"What's that?" asked Wendy.

"**Their credibility as a profession with the investing public!**" Sam replied.

"I agree!" said Steve.

"Why?" asked Debra.

Steve responded, "The world of business and finance changes so fast that it outstrips the ability of the accounting rule makers to keep pace. As a result, financial statements have become misleading—old rules do not adequately reflect the changed world. For example, new computer and communications technology outdates equipment faster than anyone expects. As a consequence, equipment depreciation is severely understated on income statements and 'one time' charge-offs surprise investors.......Another example: foreign exchange rate movements and global competition can render an industry in any given country uncompetitive—even unviable—within a few short years, resulting in bankruptcies."

Wendy added, "Steve's right! **And compounding the problem is that incredibly smart people like investment bankers, tax attorneys and international tax specialists—not to mention managers themselves—are paid big bonus money to aggressively find ways around the GAAP rules.** New financial instruments are intentionally designed to arbitrage accounting and tax rules—to shift income from one period to another while in many cases reducing cash flow."

"Yes!" said Sam, "**But the issue of the accountant's credibility goes beyond re-engineering** the spreading of historic costs in **the current financial statements. Accountants need to rethink** who the customer is for financial statements, what **the customer needs and what new concepts can be used to credibly fill the customers' needs!**.......The existing financial statements no longer even fill the needs of creditors and regulators—as evidenced by the number of rapid, 'surprise' bankruptcies of investment grade companies. The financials certainly *do not* fulfill the Shareowner needs. **Shareowners want to know if the company is earning its cost of capital,**......and, how much more or less than the cost of capital!.......**To do this, the accountants need to think outside the box of the existing historic cost spreading paradigm and the constraints of the existing three financial statements** (the income statement, balance sheet and cash flow).......**In light of advances in capital markets theory and valuation techniques, and to fulfill Shareowners' needs, the accountants need to come up with a GAAP 'Valuation Statement'!**"

Sam paused and the group waited........

In the firelight Sam continued to look concerned, and the firelight made him look a little older as he said,......"**But beyond the issue of the accountants' credibility, I think that there are two much more important issues in the balance.**"......

Everyone listened intently as Sam continued. "**The first issue is a financial markets issue.** Anything which causes investors, and other capital market participants to loose confidence in the credibility of financial information, jeopardizes the liquidity and efficiency of capital markets—i.e. the ability to raise debt and equity in order to finance new ideas and job growth!"......

Sam looked at Susan Perrier, "**The second issue is a socio-economic issue.** As the world population grows, resources are increasingly scarce. Each generation has a responsibility to use resources as efficiently as possible both for its own benefit as well as to leave more for future generations. **We need to focus management on effectively creating economic value (i.e. Enterprise Value),** *not* **on managing the accounting numbers which often results in proactive destruction of economic value!**"

Susan Perrier, the manager from the Environmental Protection Agency perked her ears up at this. She was quietly biding her time waiting for an opportunity to discuss things other than economic issues......She continued her patient wait;......stalking, so to speak........

"I agree with Sam," said Ed. "Financial statements are riddled with unusual items and one time charges related to management discretion in applying accounting standards. The recent change in accounting for goodwill in acquisitions[10] is going to make earnings comparison techniques such as sales, earnings or EPS growth rates and P/E's almost useless to investors in determining the value of a company......In fact, **based upon our conversations the past few days, I believe that the new accounting standard for acquisitions will promote increased destruction of Economic Profit and Enterprise Value.**"

An obviously frustrated and concerned, Georgia commanded, "Explain!"

---

10. FAS No. 142, Goodwill and Other Intangible Assets

Ed replied, "If Company A pays $100mm to acquire Company B, and if Company B has assets such as plants and trademarks only worth $40mm, then Company A is said to have paid $60mm ($100mm–$40mm) for Goodwill. Under the old accounting rule, this $60mm of Goodwill would have been expensed in the income statement over say 30 years and would reduce pretax earnings by $2 mm per year. Under the new accounting rule, unless it is 'impaired', Goodwill is not expensed, and therefore, accounting income is higher by $2mm per year. From a comparability viewpoint, this GAAP accounting change aligned US accounting with international practice. However, the result will be that in the absence of the Goodwill expense, management, either naively or thinking that their Shareowners are naive, will spend more to buy other companies to add sales and earnings to the Income Statement—i.e. ostensibly to 'grow the company'!.......**The reality is that many of these new acquisitions will not even earn the WACC and will be destroying—not growing—Enterprise Value!**......*To avoid misleading Shareowners to an even greater extent, the accountants must introduce a Valuation Statement!*"

"That's a strong statement!" said Debra.........."No pun intended!"

"Yes!" said Ed, "But I don't think that I'll be proven wrong! As we heard earlier this week, 70% of major acquisitions destroy Enterprise Value even though the current accounting rules expense Goodwill through the income statement on many of these acquisitions! **Under the new GAAP rules, where Goodwill doesn't have to be expensed through the income statement, management will feel that they can pay an even higher price for acquisitions. This will destroy even more Enterprise Value.......Remember! Most management incentives are paid to achieve accounting targets like EPS or Net Income.......Most incentives are not paid based on increases in Economic Profit or Enterprise Value!**"

"How would a 'Valuation Statement' pick up any of these changes sooner or *prevent* destruction of Enterprise Value?" asked Debra.

Wendy replied, "It often takes several years for management to conclude that an investment in technology is out dated, and even then, they are paid a bonus for increasing EPS, not for taking an earnings charge to write-off the old equipment. However, a Valuation Statement based on Economic Profit could be designed to almost immediately reveal that cash was not coming in the door to pay for—or to produce—an Economic Profit on the original equipment. The problem would be manifested immediately in the form of lower Economic Profit in the Valuation Statement."

Wendy continued, "Destruction of Enterprise Value at the time of acquisitions in most cases will be prevented simply by the existence of a GAAP Valuation Statement."

"Whoa!" said Debra. "Isn't that a pretty big leap of faith?"

"Not really." said Wendy. "Management typically prepares proforma forecasts of the GAAP statements before they do an acquisition in order to see what they will have to report and explain to creditors and Shareowners. If a public, audited Valuation Statement existed, they would do proformas of the Valuation Statement as part of their 'due diligence'. As a result, they would see that their high acquisition price would destroy Enterprise Value, and that they would have to explain that to Shareowners on future Valuation Statements!"

"I'll bet they would be reluctant to do that!" said Tom.

"I would think so!" replied Wendy.

"You see," said Sam, "unless the accountants provide Shareowners with easy access to standardized valuation data, the value and credibility of accounting statements for Shareowners will decline even further.......There are already liquidity impacts and lower individual share prices on the capital markets because of poor data for Shareowners. This will result in less capital to finance new ideas, lower share prices due to safety margins required by investors, and in the longer run, lower standards of living for both us and our grandchildren!"

"That's true!" said Georgia. "If people will only buy stock with higher safety margins built into P/E or PEG ratios, the value of our retirement fund will be much lower."

Heads nodded in agreement amidst dissatisfied murmurs.

After a moment, Steve observed, "Abraham Lincoln once said, 'You can fool all of the people some of the time, and some of the people all of the time, but you can't fool all of the people all of the time.'......It sounds to me like all of us have been fooling ourselves, and it's time for some of us to stop playing the fool!"

"You're right!" said Sam. "It's time for a person wearing the 'Black Mask and White Hat'!"

Cheers went up,......and from the shadows of the campfire came an ambitious, but unpracticed, attempt at whistling familiar chords from the William Tell Overture.

32.

The Prize:
..........Who will wear the
White Hat?

Sam took the interlude of whistling, cheering and good-natured hooting to pour some coffee for everyone and to pass around the oatmeal raisin cookies. He took several.......He loved oatmeal raisin cookies!....And Terry made the best!

"So Sam!" said Wendy, "**Who's going to wear the White Hat?**"

"It would just be speculation!" said Sam......."But, my guess is that **it will be worn by whoever has the most to gain!**"

That evasion drew even more hoots and comments, as Sam laughed heartily and choked on his cowboy coffee.

Nancy gave him a few 'helpful', hard pats on the back, ...playfully twisted his ear,......and, like a scolding sister, mercilessly said, "**Answer the question!**"

Slowly, Sam regained his cowboy composure;......lost it;......regained it;......and continued,......"**There is a lot to be gained** here!......Money?......Yes!.......But also, political advantage, bureaucratic prestige,

231

capital market liquidity, public interest, possibly national economic leadership,......and yes,......even pride and integrity.......**There is a lot to be lost as well!**......Money,......political opportunity, bureaucratic influence, liquidity in global capital markets, national economic leadership......and even pride and integrity."

Sam continued, "**I surely hope the accountants will take the lead!......For centuries their role has been to provide creditors and Shareowners with an impartial valuation of their respective interests in the company.**......While the valuation has been imperfect, it was at least credible within reason.......As we just discussed, when the world moved slower, the income statement, cash flow and balance sheet served yeoman's duty for the interests of both creditors and Shareowners. However, with the development of efficient financial markets, advances in financial theory and information technology and the faster rate of change in the world today, these three statements no longer adequately serve Shareowners. There needs to be a fourth statement, a Valuation Statement, calculating Economic Profit and telling Shareowners how the company is doing relative to WACC (Weighted Average Cost of Capital)."

"After listening to Steve's earlier comments on the potential for conflicts and lost fees, **why would the accountants do it?**" asked Ed.

"**Pride and because it's their job!**" said Sam. "It may seem naive, but somewhere, some accountant(s) must feel loyalty to his/her profession and a personal responsibility to ensure its future credibility with the public—to 'ride for the brand'—so to speak. **It is unmistakably clear that the three existing financial statements are *increasingly misleading* when it comes to Shareowners!** Reasonable and accurate disclosures of Economic Profit and issues surrounding Enterprise Value in a new GAAP Valuation Statement would go a long way to restoring public confidence!"

"But if the accountants don't respond, who else could do it?" asked Debra.

"By themselves, probably only the Securities and Exchange Commission (SEC), and that would essentially only be with respect to companies who issue debt or equity to the public." said Sam.

"But," said Barb, "I am sure that there must be a lot of others who collectively could influence or cause a Valuation Statement to happen."

"You're right!" said Sam. "People like equity analysts, debt rating agencies, bankers, directors and even management could influence creation of a Valuation Statement. But, let me focus on the individual group that has the most to loose.......**Next to society itself, Shareowners have the most to loose.** Shareowners can do a lot to influence creation of a Valuation Statement, but like anything worthwhile, it will take work. To be successful, Shareowners will need to coordinate. Here are some thoughts on what Shareowners can do:

- Shareowners can require their broker's equity analysts to prepare company Valuation Statements for them before they invest. Otherwise, Shareowners might as well use discount brokers or index funds.

- Shareowners can ask company management in writing and at Shareowner meetings to present a Valuation Statement.

- Shareowners can write to the Financial Accounting Standards Board (FASB) and the Securities and Exchange Commission with a copy to the external auditors and CEO/CFO at the companies they own. Their letter should request development of a new Valuation Statement and suggest contents.

- Institutional Shareowners, like mutual funds, and Individual Shareowner clubs and organizations can act together to put resolutions in front of company Directors that require incentive plans, including stock option grants, to be based upon creation of Economic Profit as a proxy for Enterprise Value. **The resolution should also require annual presentation of an Acquisition Valuation Statement for the company before** any acquisition is made which is greater than 15% of the size of the company.

- Shareowners can write to the Chairman and Directors of the Federal Reserve, and the major stock exchanges suggesting the importance of a Valuation Statement to the credibility, liquidity and continued global leadership of U.S. financial markets.

- Shareowners can write to the President, Representatives and Senators in Congress advocating the importance of a Valuation Statement to the credibility, liquidity and global leadership of our financial markets as well as to efficient use of resources—especially people! Point out to the elected representatives that *managing our companies based upon creation of Enterprise Value,* (using Economic Profit as a proxy), *is a national competitive issue.* It's about our people's bread and butter! **Whichever nation makes its management processes more *effective* is going to have a national competitive advantage, just as we saw from the Quality Process in the 1980's—90's. In this sense, society has the most to win or lose!** Some nation will be the leader, and the rest will play a very tough game of catch up!"

In a puzzled voice, Tom asked, "What can government do?"

"Two things immediately come to mind." replied Sam. "*First,* the Commerce Department could create a prestigious national competitive award similar to the Baldridge Quality Award. The new award would recognize continuous creation of Economic Profit over a three to five year time period, and the use of Economic Profit based incentive plans.......In addition, while I am not an advocate of the *second* idea, it would work and might have merit in an emergency. If the government really wanted to accelerate efficient use of society's resources, it could give tax incentives for increasing Economic Profit over a three-year period of time. This would accelerate the transition to Economic Profit based measurements throughout the economy."

Mitch picked up on Sam's observations, "Your comment about competitive advantage going to the early adopter nation obviously applies equally to companies. Shouldn't it be in individual management's self interest to be the first to implement Economic Profit based incentive plans? If management waits until they see a competitor adopt it, they may have given the competition a two-year head start. That's hard to make up!"

"Yes." said Sam, "In theory, companies should want to be the early adopter Economic Profit based incentive plans. **But, because so many incentive plans are based upon accounting measures such as EPS and net income, management and Shareowner interests are only loosely aligned. Management wants the option of managing (arbitraging) the accounting rules in order to earn incentives, even though no Enterprise Value is created.......**It takes leadership, character and real courage for management to initiate a change to Economic Profit based plans which demand creation of real cash value to get a payout."

Mitch nodded thoughtfully, "I understand your point, and unfortunately, I believe that you are right. It's hard for people to walk away from low hanging fruit, even though it doesn't rightly belong to them!"

There was an awkward pause in the conversation. Finally, Barb came to the rescue.

"I think the idea of a national award for creating Economic Profit is a wonderful idea!"......said Barb, "The award would provide recognition, a standard measure of Economic Profit, and the winners would serve as benchmarks for others! I just hope that the application would be a lot simpler than the one for the Baldridge Quality Award!"

"I like the idea too!" said Steve.

"Back to earth, boys and girls!" chided Wendy. "Whether it's used by Shareowners for the mundane purpose of investing, or"......she good naturedly mocked, "by the President for a prestigious, national award, what should a Valuation Statement contain?"

Sam knew that her sarcasm was directed at him. He threw his hands in the air and with a laugh said. "OK!...OK!...I surrender!...But remember,......'Without vision, the people perish!'"

His eyes twinkled as he smiled at Wendy, and he continued, "Let's focus on the contents of a GAAP Valuation Statement for Shareowners.......I am sure that the President can design his own valuation statement for the national award!"

As he spoke, he reached for his saddlebags and to everyone's surprise pulled out a pack of laminates. I have been boiling this down for quite a while.......This laminate represents my current thinking on the subject."

As he passed out the laminates, Sam continued speaking, "This laminate presents a basic Valuation Statement. It is intended to be simple and understandable, and to capture 95% of the value with 5% of the effort. Remember that the intent of the Valuation Statement is to show the trend in Economic Profit computed from the simple formula we discussed earlier this week. Also, remember, a company doesn't necessarily have to have a positive EP in any given year, as long as the trend is strongly toward a positive EP over, say, a three year time period!"

$$\text{Economic Profit (or 'EP')} = \text{Net Operating Profit after Tax (NOPAT)}^* - (\text{Capital} \times \text{WACC})$$

* Plus material non-cash items such as goodwill amortization

As flashlights were turned on, Sam pointed to the top part of the sheet and slowly moved down the different categories as he commented with the highlights of each topic. He began explaining each topic:

- **'Cash Basis' NOPAT**: 'Cash Basis' NOPAT is a misnomer. We are not trying to restate the income statement to pure cash accounting. All we want to do is to add back the material non-cash items so that we get as close as possible to the cash income coming in the door. For example, we add back expense related to amortization of goodwill because it is a non-cash expense. We do not add back depreciation, because cash related to it is typically reinvested in replacement assets; however, this should be revisited depending on the company and as conditions change. We add back rents because they are a form of financial expense which will be addressed through the mechanism of adding back the off balance sheet lease assets to Capital. ...... Observe where NOPAT fits in the EP equation above.

"How would you handle 'one time' events such as non-recurring gains or charges?" asked Debra.

"The GAAP accounting charge related to these items would be excluded from the 'Cash Basis' NOPAT calculation" said Sam. "However, any cash from the gain or any cash cost associated with the charge would be added to (or subtracted from) the 'Cash Basis' NOPAT on a separate line . ... The reason is that the cash does create (or destroy) value even if it is only one time. By putting it on a separate line, a Shareowner can still see the trend in the ongoing business."

- *Capital*: The 'Capital' section identifies all of the capital (debt plus equity) used in the business regardless of whether it is on the balance sheet or not. The company would be required to identify the capital it is using in the form of financing, operating, and synthetic leases as well as sourced through any other off balance sheet method such as receivable discounting or asset securitization. We would also add back contingent liabilities such as guarantees, liability for letters of credit, and contingent capital contributions. It would include any subsidiary owned or controlled more than 50% as well as any contingent obligations to support affiliated companies (e.g. guarantees, equity contribution or buyback arrangements etc.—intent rather than form). 'On' or 'Off' balance sheet financing structure is NOT the criteria for including capital related to an asset in the definition of Capital. The criterion is whether the asset continues to be used in the business!....Observe where Capital fits into the EP equation."

- *Cost of Capital*: The 'Cost of Capital' section computes the WACC (Weighted Average Cost of Capital). To do that, the company must reveal the cost of each category of capital. For debt, the company would use the actual weighted debt cost after tax. The tax rate would be the combined statutory tax rate. For the cost of equity, the company would use the past 12 months US inflation rate plus 8%. This cost and methodology would be defined by the accounting standard establishing the Valuation Statement. The standard should be based upon what a broad market index earns. It would be based upon the premise that any individual equity must at least earn the long term, historical risk premium of the market to inflation. Otherwise, investors should just buy an S&P 500 index fund. I would not use Betas. Setting a pragmatic standard is the most critical issue at this point."......

Observe where the WACC fits into the EP equation!

- *Economic Profit*: The Economic Profit reveals in dollar terms how much value is being created (or destroyed) in the current year, i.e. how many dollars of 'Cash Basis NOPAT' it is earning above or below its Cost of Capital. It tells the Shareowner in dollar terms how much Economic Profit is being created (or destroyed).

- *Net Economic Return on Capital*: The Net Economic Return on Capital ('NEROC') reveals in percent terms how much value is being created or destroyed in a given year. It compares the rate of return earned in a given year to the WACC for that year. It tells a Shareowner in percent terms how much more (or less) the Board is earning on the company's investments than the cost of the money that the company is investing. If NEROC is not equal to WACC, the Enterprise Value will decrease.......NEROC is a macro indicator for the company, and should not be used to manage business units within the company. Economic Profit accomplishes that task much more effectively! The one line EP formula is much easier for front line people to operationalize, than ratios like ROCE and NEROC!

- *Financial Goals*: The Financial Goals section requires management to state their current financial goals, so that Shareowners can see what goals management is targeting, and the amount of increase being targeted for each goal.

- *Incentive Plan Design*: The section on Incentive Plan Design reveals by management layer, the types and structures of the incentive plans in which they participate including basis of payment, and amount paid in relationship to Economic Profit created. It also provides Shareowners with the expected incentive payout for each of the top 5 officers in relation to increases in Economic Profit per share and the market value per share over the incentive time period.

"Wow!' said Debra, "This Valuation Statement really provides a lot of useful information! As I look at it, I think that a worthwhile addition would be to compute the Enterprise Value assuming that the Economic Profit did not change."

"How would you do that?" asked Tom.

"Enterprise Value is equal to the beginning capital plus the present value of EP discounted at the WACC," said Debra.

She continued, "We know the capital at the end of the year, the WACC, and the Economic Profit for the year. If EP does not change (i.e. a no growth scenario), then the present value of Economic Profit is merely the current Economic Profit divided by the WACC. In other words, we capitalize the Economic Profit at the WACC......Let me show you an example! Assume that capital was $1 billion, that WACC was 9%, and that Economic Profit was $50mm. We could calculate a No Growth Enterprise Value as follows:"

'NO GROWTH' ENTERPRISE VALUE

	Year 1
Capital at Year End:	$1,000
Plus: Economic Profit divided by WACC*	555
No Growth Enterprise Value:	$1,555

* $50mm / 9%

"Debra, how would you use this?......Wouldn't this understate the Enterprise Value for most companies?" asked Steve.

"Yes," said Debra. "Because most companies do have growth, this will understate Enterprise Value. *But,* **it serves as a factual, auditable, rational data point for what the company is worth assuming no growth. It also serves as a benchmark from which management can discuss their expectations for future growth in Enterprise Value.**......The Valuation Statement could also be amplified to include a sensitivity analysis table showing constant growth rates through year 10 and the resultant Enterprise Value. Management can then comment on their expectations and reasons for growth of Economic Profit and the resulting change in Enterprise Value. Shareowners can compare this chart and management's expectations to the implicit growth rate contained in the company's market P/E ratio."

"That's powerful stuff!" observed Wendy.

"Let's add it to the Valuation Statement." recommended Steve. "I agree with Debra that it is a quantifiable, supportable, auditable and rational starting point to get people thinking about Enterprise Value."

"Done!" said Sam.

Georgia then said, "I notice that the back of the laminate contains a sheet called 'Acquisition Valuation Statement'. What is it?"

Sam responded, "As we discussed earlier this week, acquisitions are major events in the life of a company; 70% of the time, they destroy Enterprise Value! We need a way to make Boards and management visibly accountable for acquisitions, without necessarily revealing purchase price and other confidential information. This Acquisition Valuation Statement **represents an attempt at giving the Shareowners the information they need in order to ensure that the Boards and management are acting responsibly in the Shareowners interests.** It would be presented whenever a company acquires another company which is at least 15% of the size of the acquirer."

"Please explain it to us?" asked John.

"Glad to," said Sam. "The Acquisition Valuation Statement asks the acquirer to report only two things. The first is to show the acquisition's pro-forma *incremental* impact on Economic Profit for each of the next 5 calendar years, beginning with the pro-rata impact in the year of acquisition. This calculation includes all 'synergies' the acquirer expects to achieve anywhere in the consolidated acquirer. The capital used in the calculation includes the purchase price plus assumed debt (including off balance sheet debt) at a cost equal to the acquirer's WACC."

Sam continued, "The second item the acquirer must report is the net present value of the acquired company including synergies (i.e. the net present value of the Enhanced Cash Flows). The discount rate used in this calculation is the acquirer's WACC. The acquirer would present this statement at the time of acquisition as well as in its annual report. Notice that we are using the acquirer's pre acquisition WACC, as opposed to post acquisition WACC, as it is usually a more conservative (higher) discount rate at a point in time, and using it also avoids speculation on how the acquisition will be financed."

"That's pretty good!" said Wendy. "You get to see the best of both worlds and management doesn't have to reveal the purchase price, the assumed growth rates or synergies if they are sensitive to the seller or for competitive reasons. The NPV of the acquired company tells Shareowners how much the acquirer's Enterprise Value will increase (or decrease) if plans go as advertised. That calculation is, of course, based on a long term forecast, and **I assume that the accounting standard for the Acquisition Valuation Statement would define a standard annuity formula with no growth after year 10 and calculated using the cash flow in year 10 divided by the WACC**.......The other part I like is that the Economic Profit calculations in the first 5 years give Shareowners a sense that the returns will be realized beginning now, and that it helps to reduce the risk that the acquisition's returns will depend on achieving a hockey stick forecast in years 5 through 10!"

"It looks OK to me, and I can understand it!" said Georgia.

Sam replied, "Glad you see the sense in it!"

He continued, "If I were really defining the Valuation and Acquisition Valuation Statements, I would assemble a small group of CFO's, Economic Profit consultants, compensation specialists, accountants, and equity analysts among others, to propose the Statements' contents. The group would include people with real world experience in managing companies and in measuring and motivating people to efficiently create Enterprise Value. That way, the Statement design should have a better chance of motivating creation of Enterprise Value while preventing—or at least minimizing the prospects of people 'gaming' the system."

"Hey, Sam," said Georgia. "Who's going to wear the 'White Hat' and ride Silver?"

"It won't be me!" replied Sam. "I ride an Appaloosa named War Bonnet!"

They all laughed, and in the silence that followed, the melody and words of the song 'Home on the Range' drifted over from the larger campfire. Flashlights were extinguished, and Sam's contingent relaxed against their saddles and gazed at the sky, watching sparks from the fire drift to the heavens while enjoying the 'man made' serenade."

Valuation Statement

'CASH BASIS NOPAT'

	Year 1	Year 2	Year 3
Operating Profit Before Tax (from income statement):			
Plus: Amortization of Goodwill:			
Plus: Rents:			
Minus: Statutory Tax Rate*:			
Plus (or minus) After tax CASH impact of one time gains (or charges) not included in Operating Profit Before Taxes.			
'Cash Basis NOPAT':			

*The combined federal, state and local statutory tax rate in the US is about 38% assuming full absorption of excess foreign tax credits.

CAPITAL:

End of Year:

	Year 0	Year 1	Year 2	Year 3
Debt:				
Short Term:				
Long Term:				
Off Balance Sheet (including asset securitizations, operating, financial and synthetic leases, and other contingent liabilities)				
Total Debt:				
Average Debt Capital:	N/A			
Total Equity: (Based Upon Market Value):				
Average Equity Capital:	N/A			
Total Capital:				
Average Total Capital:	N/A			

COST OF CAPITAL*:

	Year 1	Year 2	Year 3
Cost of Debt (After Tax):			
Short Term:			
Long Term:			
Off Balance Sheet (including asset securitizations, operating, financial and synthetic leases, and other contingent liabilities):			
Weighted Average Cost of Debt (After Tax):			
Cost of Equity (After Tax using the calendar year Consumer Price Index plus 8% as the after tax cost):			
Weighted Average Cost of Capital (Using average debt and average market value of equity):			

*All Amounts after tax at statutory tax rate in Cash Basis NOPAT calculation

ECONOMIC PROFIT:

	Year 1	Year 2	Year 3
'Cash Basis NOPAT':			
Minus: Average Capital x WACC:			
Economic Profit:			

NET ECONOMIC RETURN ON CAPITAL ('NEROC'):

	Year 1	Year 2	Year 3
'Cash Basis NOPAT':			
Divided by: Average Capital:			
Economic Return on Capital:			
Minus: WACC:			
Net Economic Return on Capital:			

MARKET VALUE:

End of Year:

	Year 1	Year 2	Year 3
Share Price:			
Multiplied by: Outstanding Shares:			
Market Value:			

NO GROWTH ENTERPRISE VALUE:

End of Year:

	Year 1	Year 2	Year 3
Capital at Year End:			
Plus: Economic Profit divided by WACC:			
No Growth Enterprise Value:			

ENTERPRISE VALUE SENSITIVITY AND OUTLOOK:

This section includes a sensitivity analysis table showing growth rates through year 10 and the resultant Enterprise Value as well as management's comments on their expected growth rates and change in Enterprise Value.

FINANCIAL GOALS:

Provide a brief description of management's current financial goals and the rate of change anticipated in them. For example: Our goal is to increase Economic Profit 50% p.a. over the next 5 years and 25% p.a. thereafter through year 10.

INCENTIVE PLAN DESIGN:

Provide a description of incentive plans revealing by management layer, the types and structures of the incentive plans in which different groups of managers participate including basis of payment, and amount paid in relationship to Economic Profit created. The section also provides Shareowners with the expected incentive payout for each of the top 5 officers in relation to increases in Economic Profit per share and the market value per share over the incentive time period.

Acquisition Valuation Statement

Proforma Impact on Economic Profit:

	Year 1	Year 2	Year 3	Year 4	Year 5
Incremental Economic Profit					

This represents the Board's estimate of the increase in the acquirer's Economic Profit resulting from the acquisition in each of the first 5 years. It is based upon the concept of Enhanced Cash Flow, and therefore includes projected 'synergies'.

Net Present Value of Acquisition:

This represents the Board's estimate of the increase in the acquirer's Enterprise Value resulting from the acquisition, assuming no growth in the acquired company subsequent to the 10th year, and after subtracting the purchase price including assumed debt. The acquirers' current WACC is used as the discount rate. The notes here would explain the assumed growth rate, margin, synergies and WACC used in the calculations.

33.

Friday's Drive

The Wranglers were up at 4:30 on Friday, and the rest of the camp was awake and moving by 5:30. As the guests quickly discovered, waking up on the ground, getting dressed inside a bedroll, rolling up their sleeping gear and packing things up for the Chuck Truck took a little longer than just jumping out of bed in a cabin. Many of them gave the Wranglers a hand saddling the horses while others helped the 'Chef' (A title which she had now been popularly awarded!), Terry Brandon, to prepare breakfast. While there was social conversation during the chores, everyone was too occupied for Sam's Coffee Club to hold its 'regular' morning session.

After a good, dude, working breakfast of hot cakes and syrup, scrambled eggs, sausage, bacon, biscuits and coffee, everyone was ready to ride! They needed a hearty breakfast to replenish the energy they burned as they rode and herded the cattle.

The day picked up where it began Thursday. This time it was Chisholm's role to command 'Head 'em Up!…Move 'em Out!' followed by drovers' whips providing resounding 'Whhhaaackkks!'

During the course of the morning, Fletcher found Elk and mule deer tracks, while Jose found more sign of bear. They saw several hawks and an eagle soar overhead.

About mid morning the herd crossed a stream whose banks were filled with signs of small animals that had come to drink. A little before 11:30, the herd stopped by a beaver dam. The drovers enjoyed a short break and ate the sandwiches they carried in their saddlebags. The guests marveled at the engineering skill and work ethic of the beaver community. Thirty minutes after they stopped, they were back in the saddle pushing the herd toward the final two passes to Sweet Pasture.

Finally, at 1:30 p.m. they rode over the last pass and looked out through a picture book mountain vista. Beyond the steep tree covered sides of the pass, they could see a giant meadow about five miles long and two miles wide situated with mountains on the west and a border of Aspen trees and Engelmann Spruce on the north. A steep drop off formed the eastern boundary. Closer to the south end of the meadow, they could see a 40 acre lake fed by a mountain stream. The overflow from the lake created another small stream meandering through the meadow. Cheers went up from the young people when they saw the campsite with the Chuck Truck already set up. The cattle seemed to sense that they were almost home, and they even seemed to move faster down the trail to Sweet Pasture.

By the time that the cattle were comfortably situated in the meadow, Glen and some of the wranglers had set up solar showers and the adult guests made prompt use of them. Nicholas and Fletcher went down to the lake and incoming stream. During the remainder of the afternoon, Nicholas proceeded to catch several Rainbow and Brown Trout, and with Fletcher's netting technique, they landed and kept three trout for dinner including one at 28" and two at 24". Glen helped them clean the fish, and Terry Brandon promised to prepare them in her special mountain seasoning together with lemon, butter and bacon.

After showers and a change of clean clothes, a few of the adults took an afternoon nap while Emma, Paige, Alexa and some of the teenagers practiced simulated barrel racing around bushes with Dakota, Gina and Marianne. It was still about two hours until supper, so when members of Sam's Coffee Club saw Sam sitting on top of a knoll several hundred yards above the camp, they decided to take their cameras and drinks to join him.

34.

Responsibility to Future Generations!

When the 'Coffee Club' members arrived on the knoll where Sam sat, the serenity and marvelous panorama quickly subdued their conversation. Sam was seated on a small rock formation under the shade of several Ponderosa Pines and Aspen. The small one-acre knoll was blanketed with Crimson Sage, Raspberry Aster and yellow Alpine Sunflowers mingled with Colorado's state flower, the blue and white Blue Columbine. As they looked out from the knoll they saw a series of high country meadows separated by brief tree lines and curving in a giant arc along the edge of a canyon a thousand feet deep. On the canyon floor a glistening stream flowed northeast.

Sam greeted them, "Welcome to Paul Bunyan's golf course!"……Suddenly the pastures transformed themselves into fairways, and the canyon into a world-class hazard. "Have a seat!" he said as he motioned to the rock outcroppings in the shade. He patted the stone beside him and beckoned Susan Perrier to join him.

"This is what it must have looked like to the Native Americans and mountain men!" he said as he waived his arm over the top of the world. "It's a heritage worth preserving!"

For the next 15 minutes, they all quietly sipped their water and Gatorade and lost themselves in daydreams.

Finally, Sam turned to Susan and said, "Susan, you have been very patient with us as we talked about Enterprise Value this week.......Thank you for your courtesy!......But, during the past few days, your eyes told me that you have some doubts and questions. Would you like to share them with us?"

Susan hadn't expected to be asked for her concerns, and she was caught a little off guard. But, she wasn't about to miss the opportunity! "Thank you for asking, Sam! When you look out on this grand view and talk about a heritage worth preserving, you are touching subjects very dear to me.......I joined the Environmental Protection Agency because I wanted to help people live well, but do it in a safe, healthy way both for ourselves and for future generations. In trying to do that, I have seen so many situations where companies have wasted or destroyed nature for generations to come in the pursuit of profits. I am wary when someone talks about making even more profit. How do my concerns reconcile with the pursuit of Economic Profit and Enterprise Value?"

"That's a very legitimate......*and* responsible ...... question!" acknowledged Sam......."I'll be up front with you and concede that **no corporate measurement or incentive system can replace balanced judgment or individual responsibility** for the impact a company's actions have on all of its constituents—including the community, the environment and future generations. **Numbers can't do that! Only leadership and leaders with character can do it!**"

"Having said that," he continued, "some incentive plans cause people to focus more on the present than on the future. For example, incentive plans based on accounting numbers such as EPS or net income, and plans based upon discrete fixed time periods such as a three years, usually cause people to minimize accounting expense in the current period.......They do this without regard for the fact that spending money now could prevent, or minimize major expense later to clean up or to fix an even bigger problem."

"I believe that properly designed Economic Profit based incentive plans cause people to accept greater responsibility for the future by helping people understand and quantify how the future impacts the present.......As an example, Economic Profit based incentive plans have two useful features compared to GAAP accounting based incentive plans.......*First*, there is training to teach people that the Enterprise Value of a company is the net present value of all future cash flows. That means people are taught that failure to invest now to prevent a problem, could produce a major cash cost to fix the problem in the future. The future cash cost has a current, quantifiable impact on the company's Enterprise Value—the thing that managers are being paid to increase!......The **training has merit! People learn that the future has quantifiable value in the present!**......*Second*, the Economic Profit incentive plan serves as the proxy for Enterprise Value, and is tied to a *rolling* **three-year bonus pool.** The *rolling* feature means that employees keep incentive money that they have earned at risk indefinitely into the future. If they do something today which saves money, but it results in larger costs in the future, employees know that they will loose some of the bonus pool that they have built up by reducing costs in the earlier years."

Mitch asked, "Can't you accomplish much the same thing by using three year EPS or net income pools?"

Sam responded, "No, they don't capture the cost of capital, and they have all of the accounting distortions which we are trying to eliminate or minimize by going to a 'Cash Basis NOPAT'."

Susan interjected, "Sam, **if leadership is the answer, why do you need to change to Enterprise Value and Economic Profit based plans at all?"**

"Excellent question, Susan!" replied Sam.......The answer is that **even leaders need the right conceptual framework to make good decisions**.......When leaders and managers are making decisions about a company, they need a conceptual model which is comprehensive in measuring all the resources used, including capital, and a model that gives them a correct understanding of how future actions affect the present value of the company, and vice versa.......They also need to understand that **by creating value for Shareowners, the company survives and creates value for its other constituents including employees and the community.** The Enterprise Value model gives a comprehensive, simple way to assess various outcomes of a decision.......**Once the leader knows the impact on Enterprise Value, s/he can then judge whether some other quantifiable or non-quantifiable good (or harm) to another constituent should outweigh the economic impact on the company.......Decisions are usually much easier once a person has the facts in the right format!**"

Sam continued, "The Enterprise Value model helps a decision maker to have a clear forward looking picture of the impact of his decision on a company over a number of years. For company managers, paid with rolling incentive plans, it shows them how incurring expense or investing capital today may prevent them from loosing or investing much more money in the future. Admittedly, this is just one of the inputs to a decision, but it helps to eliminate rhetoric and hypothesis which surround one year snapshots. The decision maker can then look at other factors with more certainty of the total impact of his decision on the company as well as other constituents."

"I understand what you are saying." said Susan. "Better conceptual models, better training and better incentive plans help managers to make better decisions. But, in the end, even with the best financial models and incentive plans, it still comes back to a human decision!"

"That's exactly right!" said Sam. "A human decision born out of knowledge, character, leadership and integrity.........or the absence of these qualities!"

"I'd like to talk about leadership!" said Barb.

As Lone Eagle walked up to the group and sat down on a rock beside her, Wendy said, "I would like to talk about character and integrity as well! As we rode together these past two days, Lone Eagle has raised issues causing me to think that character and integrity, not generic leadership or incentive models, are what will cause the right decisions to be made."

"Sounds like a must topic!" said Nancy.

Sam smiled, slowly turned, nodded at Lone Eagle, looked back at Barb and said, "I can't think of a better place to discuss leadership than sitting right here at the top of the world with the perspective that a view like this brings!"

35.

Character:
The 'sine qua non' of Leadership!

"Where do you begin a topic like leadership?" asked Barb.

"There's *only* one place!" Sam said slowly.

"Where's that?" asked Debra.

"With character!" replied Sam.

As the wind conveyed his idea to the group, Sam continued to silently survey the landscape and 70 mile horizon lying in front of him.

Three minutes of silence passed among the group.

Finally, Nancy broke it like the crisp report of a rifle.

"You're right!" said Nancy. "Popular definitions of leaders include people like George Washington, John Adams, Abraham Lincoln, Winston Churchill, Martin Luther King, Margaret Thatcher, and Rosa Parks; they also include Stalin, Hitler and Sadam Hussein.......But, I wouldn't put these two groups of people in the same leadership category.......**Leadership has to be more than just having a vision, persuading people to understand it and motivating people to achieve it**—all of these people did that!.....**Leadership is also about what the vision is—the trail's end—and the methods used to get there! The end** must be worthwhile, but in addition, even good ends don't justify bad means!......I think that it must be *character* which helps to define 'good' ends and acceptable methods of achieving them!"

"I understand your premise, and I agree with it," said Ed. "But, how do you define character?"

Lone Eagle spoke up. "Character is about having a set of worthwhile values and the courage to live them. The values begin with integrity, which I define as the self-discipline to be honest with both yourself and others and to keep your word—not just the letter of your word, but also the spirit of your word. Character includes other worthwhile values such as respect for others and nature as well as for ideas like the equality of all people and their right to life, liberty and the pursuit of happiness. Character encompasses courage. Not only courage to lead, because leadership is lonely, but also, the willingness—the 'backbone'— to take personal risks to do and say the things which are unpopular because they are right to do!.......And, character involves loyalty; not just loyalty to institutions or to people, but also loyalty to ideas which form the basis for relationships between people, and which connect one generation to the next."

Lone Eagle paused and looked at Sam.

Sam picked up the conversation, "Lone Eagle, you said it well beyond your years!.........Character is the 'sine qua non' ('without which none!') of Leadership! It's essence is partially embodied in old western phrases, like 'A man's word is his bond', 'He rides for the brand' and a newer one 'Scout's Honor.' They mean something to the people who live by them and to the people who know those who live by them."

"But why is character so important to Shareowners and companies?" asked Jim Perrier.

Sam paused and responded, "Do you remember the movie 'Patton' starring George C. Scott?"

The group members nodded.

Sam continued, "There was a scene in the movie where General Patton, portrayed by George C. Scott, was surveying a battlefield in which US tanks had just beaten back a German advance in a costly battle. As I recall, the battle occurred near a line of concrete bunkers built by the French along their eastern border with Germany. The bunkers had heavy cannon that only pointed west in order to defend against a German invasion.......The Germans had come around the north end of the line of bunkers and attacked from its rear. As he viewed the fixed French fortifications known as the Maginot line, Patton was quoted as saying:

> Fixed fortifications are monuments to the stupidity of man! For if God's mountain ranges and oceans can be overcome, then anything built by man can be overcome!

"**Herein lie the fundamental weaknesses of any company, any incentive plan, any regulation or any accounting rule.** A company may have the best accounting systems, the best-defined financial goals, and the best designed incentive plans, but **they are only man made rules.......**As such, they have flaws. First, the rule writers can't anticipate every contingency or every way that a motivated person can find to get around them. Second, the rules are essentially static—or 'fixed'—relative to the speed with which this dynamic world changes. Third, mankind is governed by natural laws—including the one that states that all matter seeks its lowest energy level—until stimulated! People will always try to get around the rules, if it is easier than living by them. They will do it 'legally' and usually in good conscience, but they will do it!......And finally, rules only exist to the extent that a leader disciplines the company and says that it is going to live by the rules.......**It takes leaders with character to ensure that the organization lives up to the spirit of the rules, as well as the letter of the rules, because there will always be 'loopholes' or 'exceptions'.......**To look out for their interests, Shareowners need more than just managers,......more than just leaders,......they need leaders with character who will ensure that the companies do right by the Shareowner as well as other constituents, in spite of the many, easier opportunities for the manager to do otherwise."

As Sam paused, Wendy spoke up, "Yesterday, as we rode, Lone Eagle commented on the importance of the character of the CEO and CFO. Can you speak to that?"

Sam nodded 'yes' as he paused thoughtfully.......'As the principal company managers, the CEO and the CFO are the fiduciaries for the Shareowners. Their first duty is to represent the people who hired them, who entrusted their hard earned money to the company, but who cannot be present to represent themselves.......The buck stops with the CEO and CFO when it comes to setting the example in representing the Shareowner's interests.......As the nominal leaders of a company, the CEO and CFO set the culture of the company—the way that people act in the absence of written procedures or rules.......In this regard, **the distance between the leaders and the followers is a constant.** Given the same circumstances, different CEOs/CFOs will get different results from the same group of people.......The character underlying their leadership is multiplied and reflected in the people who follow them, and therefore, dramatically impacts the value created (or destroyed) for Shareowners as well as other constituents."......

"Sam!......Sam!" interrupted an agitated Steve, "Sam!......I have to stop you!......You are being too gentle!....Let me say it from the perspective of a CFO who is upset by the lack of character and integrity demonstrated in visible actions of many CFO's and in CEO's in two key areas!"

"You have the podium!" said Sam with a smile.

"Thanks! Sorry to interrupt, but I feel strongly about this!" said Steve.

Steve began, "The CEO and CFO are just like any other cowboy! They are hired hands! The traits of character and integrity argue that they owe 'loyalty to the brand' including 'a fair day's work for a fair day's pay'. As you said, Sam, in the context of a company, the brand is the Shareowner, and they work for the brand through the company."

He continued, "**The CEO and CFO's first responsibility to the brand—the Shareowner—is to have the intellectual integrity to understand what their job is; and, that means to understand how value is created for the Shareowner.** To do that the CEO and CFO must be as conversant in Economic Profit, Enterprise Value and WACC as they are in FASB GAAP rules. I am shocked by how many CEO's—let alone CFO's—don't know their company's cost of capital (WACC), and don't understand that their job is to earn more than the WACC in order to increase the Enterprise Value.......Everything that the CEO and CFO do for the company, including setting the company culture and establishing the company Value Circle, begins with a fundamental understanding of what their job is!"

Steve gave a wry smile, "My second point relates to integrity in pay. **Once the CEO and CFO understand that the company's job is to create Enterprise Value, then character demands that they install financial measures and incentive plans which pay people for creating Economic Profit and not for 'gaming' the system by playing with the accounting rules!** As I said, the CEO/CFO and the management team are hired hands......plain and simple. They chose the relative security of working for a company rather than betting their money on a grub steak and going it on their own to search for gold like an entrepreneur. As a result, they have a right to competitive pay, but, they don't have the right like a gold miner to a bonanza! They haven't taken the capital risk!......Integrity in structuring incentive plans means to pay management based upon what they control—Economic Profit. The incentive plans should not be a function of the serendipity of supply and demand for stock price."

At this point Ed jumped in. " Steve, you haven't minced any words, and I won't either."

"I wouldn't expect you to!" joked Steve.

Ed laughed. "This week has been an eye opener for me. As I reflect on what I have learned about Economic Profit and Enterprise Value and relate it to the issues of character and integrity, I begin to see how transparent actions of CEO's and CFO's are, if you know what to look for."

With a grin Ed said. "In your own subtle way Steve, you have helped me to understand why so many CEO's and CFO's use the old eight envelope style of management."

"What's that?" asked Georgia.

"Well," said Ed, "It seems that a new CEO had been appointed to run a company. As he prepared for his new duties, the new CEO asked the outgoing CEO for advice on how to deal with the Board of Directors whenever problems arose. The outgoing CEO having prepared for this question, handed the new CEO eight envelopes numbered 1 through 8. The old CEO said, 'Whenever you have a problem with the Board, open an envelope, beginning with number 1.'"

......"Six months later the Board was concerned over profits and asked the new CEO what the problem was. He excused himself from the meeting and opened the first envelope. It said 'Blame the old CEO.' So, the new CEO went back into the Board meeting and blamed the old CEO for the problem. The Board was understanding and said OK."......

"Almost every six months thereafter, the same question of profits arose, and each time the new CEO excused himself from the Board meeting, opened the next envelope and told the Board that he was going to do what it said. The envelopes and their counsel read as follows:

- Envelope #2: Reorganize the company;
- Envelope #3: Cut costs;
- Envelope #4: Use management discretion, and change the way accounting rules are applied to the company by saying that you've benchmarked what other companies are doing, and 'are just conforming to what your competitors are doing';
- Envelope #5: Make acquisitions to 'grow';

- Envelope #6: Divest businesses and sell assets in order to take gains on the sales and 'reduce operating expenses';
- Envelope #7: Take a one time accounting charge to get rid of 'unneeded assets'.

"Finally, the new CEO had to retire to his office to open Envelope #8.......He did so slowly.......As he read it, his chin dropped to his chest because it said, 'Prepare eight envelopes!'"

Everyone laughed.

Ed said, "While this story has humor, it gets at a sad truth. Historically, equity analysts, Boards and many Shareowners have mistaken motion for movement in the right direction.......After this week, I have a new theme: '**Motion that doesn't get results** (in the form of increased Economic Profit and Enterprise Value) **is called commotion!**'......We need the Valuation Statement that we've discussed to provide essential information to Shareowners and Boards as well as to discipline, train and bring backbone to CEO's, CFO's and Boards."

As Ed finished speaking, there was silence and some faces reflected introspection.

The leaves rustled in the mild afternoon breeze.

After a few minutes, Barb smiled and said, "I have a thought which a friend shared on how to bring character into decisions.......My friend said, 'Make your decisions in a way that you would be proud to explain them to you grandchildren if they read about the decision in a newspaper the next morning.'"

"Good idea!" said John.

"Let me share another insight." said Wendy. "I recently heard a high school senior define 'character' in a speech to 1,200 school mates during a National Honor Society induction ceremony. She said, 'Character happens when a person only has to answer to themselves, and decides to personally sacrifice in order to do the right thing!'"......

Wendy continued, "It kind of reminds me of a cowboy out by himself on the wide, lonesome range,......'Doing a fair days work for a fair day's pay!' because that's what he signed on to do, no matter how tough it gets!......And because, as Marianne said, 'She can't quit a horse!'"

Sam listened to the short silence, then said, "A broader understanding of Economic Profit and Enterprise Value will make it easier for CEO's and CFO's to represent the Shareowner's interests. However, character is an attribute that will always be in short supply—and even with high demand, it's something that can't be bought!......Character puts backbone and meaning into Leadership!"

After some more moments of silence, Sam said, "Lone Eagle, perhaps you should have the last word on this subject."

Lone Eagle looked at Sam, and with a nod of thanks said, "My grandfather taught me that **when you study a man's tracks and his words, you are also looking into a man's heart. If the man cannot be honest with himself about where his tracks have led, then he cannot be honest with others.**"......

Lone Eagle concluded, "**No other qualities in a person can replace character and integrity.**"

It was quiet.

Suddenly everyone's attention was drawn to the camp.......The dinner bell was ringing, beckoning hungry wranglers to food.......Everyone picked up their canteens, and Sam mounted his Appaloosa and walked War Bonnet down the hill alongside the group.

That evening, the cowboys and cowgirls downed a wonderful steak dinner and enjoyed cowboy songs (not country western songs) sung by Will Dudley. Will was a Vietnam veteran from Walsenburg, Colorado who like a troubadour of old wanted to preserve the great heritage of cowboy songs. Emma liked 'Yellow Rose of Texas' and 'Cool Clear Water', but she also loved a song that Will had written for kids called 'Itty Bitty Outlaw'. Sam also awarded the guests a very special hand woven leather La Reata ('lariat') as a remembrance of the cattle drive to Sweet Pasture, and he gave each of them one of Will's CD's filled with cowboy songs for cold, winter nights.

About 10:30, the camp became silent as tired drovers wrapped themselves in sleeping bags to ward off the night's chill.

As she lay in her sleeping bag looking up at a million stars in the crystal black sky, Wendy recalled Lone Eagle's words, "Nothing can replace character and integrity."

She fell asleep, listening as the wind carried the acappella of a distant, lone wolf delivering a sharp, clear soliloquy.

Part VII

Roundup!

36.

Roundup!

The return from Sweet Pasture began early on Saturday. Perhaps the guests were anxious to see family, or perhaps it was the prospect of a soft bed at the home ranch, but in any event, everyone had breakfast and was in the saddle by 7:00. Friendly farewells were said to Chisholm and Glen who planned to stay with the herd for a few days to ensure that the cattle were settled in to their new pasture. Lone Eagle, Fletcher and Nicholas took the lead as they began the 17-mile ride back to the ST Lodge. They talked scouting and fishing the whole way back. Marianne rode with Emma and the other young people pointing out different birds and flowers and during one break, she showed them how to throw a rope. Sam and Wendy rode together, and in pastures would ride up beside other couples to share conversation. It was a lovely, high country day and a scenic ride!

After arriving at the home ranch at about noon, they all had lunch by the pool, and then, broke to clean up and pack up for the next day's departures.

His Saturday chores done, 3 p.m. found Sam napping on a porch chair in the cool shade. He woke with a 'start' at 3:30 as an ice-cold can of Pepsi Cola was lightly, but firmly touched to his cheek in the hand of an impishly smiling Wendy.

Nancy greeted him in that fondly admonishing, sisterly tone, and saying, "SAM McALLEN......It's time for you to pay attention to your guests! WAKE UP!"

Sam slowly pushed his hat back to reveal a big, sheepish grin, and took his feet off the rail as he reached for the Pepsi. As he looked at Wendy and Nancy he said, "By golly, where would an old cowboy be without the two of you keeping him on his feet?"

"Probably out on the range doing something useful!" deadpanned Nancy.

"Like taking a siesta!" added Steve.

There were more than a few chuckles, and Sam realized that he was surrounded by his Coffee Club. This time they were all seated with iced tea or sodas in their hands instead of coffee.

"We just came by to say thanks, and to give you the type of 'wakeup' call that you've given some of us this week," laughed Barb.

"Well, shucks!" said Sam, "If there were any wakeup calls, I think that a bright group of people like this probably gave it to themselves!......But, now that you bring it up, I am curious as to what you discovered this week. Perhaps some of you would be willing to share with us."

"Are you sure?" said Georgia with a quizzical smile.

"I'm sure." smiled Sam, as he blinked some sleep out of his eyes.

"This will be fun!" said Debra.

"OK, I'll go first!" said Georgia.

Then with larceny in her eye, and tongue in cheek, she said, "I learned that there weren't any silver bullets!"

Georgia was immediately interrupted by more than a few moans from the audience; and the comments, "Low blow!......Get the hook!" were heard several times.

Georgia and Sam feigned studying each other warily, and then began laughing together.

"OK!…OK!…I'll go straight!" she said……."The most important financial lesson I learned this week is that creating value in a company is no different than in my personal life; it all has to do with cash!……In order to create economic value for myself, I have to earn more than the cost of the money I invest. In order to create value for Shareowners, company managers have to earn more than the cost of the capital that they invest."

Tom followed his wife's comments, " Georgia and I also discovered that there are three things which cause stock prices to change:

1. The cash flow of the company;
2. The company's cost of capital; and,
3. Supply and demand for the company's stock."

"The first two determine the net present value of cash flow, which is called Enterprise Value. The Enterprise Value is the value around which the market price fluctuates—even though supply & demand factors may temporarily move the market price away from Enterprise Value. The market price is like water, constantly seeking to find its lowest level; Enterprise Value is like a magnet which keeps attracting the stock price from any level to itself."

Following Tom's comment, Patty Perrier volunteered, "For the first time, I became aware that *two* people are responsible for creating Shareowner Value……The Shareowner, and the company managers!"

"And,"……said Jim Perrier, "along with Patty, for the first time I understand the role of the Shareowner and the company managers in creating Shareowner Value……Shareowners are responsible for determining the price at which they buy and sell the stock, and managers are responsible for creating (or destroying) Enterprise Value—the net present value of cash flow. If Shareowners want to reliably create value for themselves, they should buy a company below its Enterprise Value per share, and sell when its price is above Enterprise Value per share.......One way to accomplish that is to buy at a 'PEG' ratio less than 1.......But, to do it right, we need a Valuation Statement that gives Shareowners better information in order to estimate the Enterprise Value."

"I enjoyed the lessons learned from the 'Old Trail Bosses', which Jose brought to life!" said John. " I especially like the idea of the 'Lead Steer', and the way Jose related it to Economic Profit........The concept of Economic Profit is so basic that we overlook its elegance.......EP really is like a global positioning navigation system ('GPS') that tells you exactly where you are. EP simply determines whether on a cash basis, a company is earning more dollars than the cost of the invested capital.......And, as in navigation, it is easy to see why three GPS points—or three years of EP calculations—show a trend, which reveals whether a company is making progress toward creating (or destroying) Enterprise Value."

Debra sat forward in her chair, and added her observations on the week, "It was good for me to step back from the academic environment and to listen to comments which Steve, Jose and Sam made about competition and motivation. I was reminded that to create Shareowner Value—by any definition -, a company has to compete in a very dynamic world. Jose's goal pyramid was thought provoking!..... And, after considering it, I agree with Jose that making Enterprise Value a company's primary goal will result in a renewal culture that causes a company to reinvent itself and adapt to a changing competitive landscape. ....Thinking about competition from a 'product' perspective, I also agree that using Economic Profit as a 'Lead Steer' will change how a company creates product offerings, as well as, the way a company competes........Economic Profit really can be an industry revolutionizing model!"

Mitch leaned forward in his chair and added. "As I listened to Jose present the Value Circle, I was reminded that the real purpose of incentive plans is to direct and motivate people in the creation of Enterprise

Value.......In the rush of everyday work, I had forgotten that!......I was also reminded that to do a world-class job of directing and motivating people, Human Resources needs to proactively work with the CEO and CFO to define the Value Circle. Completing all four points on the Value Circle is essential to effectively creating Enterprise Value.......And, that is really what we are being hired and paid to do!......Barb asked earlier this week 'What causes Value to happen?' I am now convinced that Jose's answer is correct........Completing the Value Circle is critical to *causing* value to happen!"

Jose offered a comment, "I am pleased to have been able to share something useful with all of you!......But, as I was doing it, I also was learning!......As we talked about models and formulas this week, it occurred to me that in the end, we do not want to create 'Digital Managers' who like 'Digital Actors' are simply products of some computer program and who simply do what the computer formulas tell them to do. We need thoughtful leaders with character who understand their role and who understand that it can't all be put in writing. They have to live their responsibilities to the Shareowner with a fundamental commitment to creating Enterprise Value in every decision.......And, they have to let others see them living that commitment!......That's part of leadership!"

At this point Ed Rogers shifted in his chair, and then volunteered, "I will be leaving the ranch with a renewed appreciation of my role.......In many respects my access to management, makes my role unique. I need to focus on asking questions that determine if management really does understand that its job is to create Enterprise Value. I also, need to communicate with investors whether management's answers to these questions are consistent with the tracks that the company is leaving in the form of trends in Economic Profit.......When acquisitions are pending, I also am in a unique position to push management to produce the information on Sam's Acquisition Valuation Statement before the acquisition is done.......I agree with Wendy that if you pay too much, no acquisition is a good one. The best way to avoid the destruction of Enterprise Value caused by paying too much for an acquisition is to avoid overpaying in the first place!"......Ed then took some poetic license as he said,......"As Sam and Lone Eagle will tell you, in the end, there aren't enough fools out there to bail out all the other fools!"

That got a two-minute belly laugh out of everyone!......

That laughter, and a warm, gentle, summer breeze that blew across the porch, stirred Steve from a deep reverie. He decided to contribute his thoughts to the group, "Last evening as I lay awake in my sleeping bag listening to the simultaneous resonance and silence of nature in the high mountains, I thought back to stories from my youth. One in particular stood out. It was Hans Christian Andersen's story about *The Emperor's New Clothes*.......Recall, it is the story of the vain Emperor who loved new clothes, and who paid two bags of gold to two rogues to weave the fabric for a new suit. They worked diligently night and day on looms, and in the process they asked for many bags of gold yarn to complete the suit. After many days, the emperor ordered the sensible Prime Minister to view the suit's progress. As he watched the busy rogues, they spoke of the fabric's softness and beautiful texture. But, the Prime Minister could see nothing on the looms! Not wanting to appear stupid or incompetent, he said, 'What marvelous fabric! I'll certainly tell the Emperor!'......As you know, the story evolved until the Emperor wore his new suit in a parade for all his subjects to see. As the Emperor rode in the parade, he heard courtiers and villagers who supplied the court praise the color and contour of his new suit—even though they could see nothing!......He also soon heard the voice of a small boy.......The boy had no important job. But, the boy did have clear vision and a clear voice.......The young boy repeated the truth again and again, 'The Emperor has no clothes!'"

Steve took a sip of iced tea and continued. "From the perspective of Shareowners, GAAP accounting has no clothes! And capital market theorists, lost in theoretical, micro minutiae have not been helpful in distilling the essence of capital markets theory so that it can be combined with accounting to measure if companies are earning more than their cost of capital!......The time has come for a practical approach to the problem.......I agree with Sam, that the practical approach begins with the development of a Valuation Statement and an Acquisition Valuation Statement together with standards similar to what we discussed this week.......The time has come!......Too many people are being deceived and hurt by the absence of clear thinking in measuring the creation (or destruction) of Enterprise Value!"

There was a brief silence.

"Wow!" exclaimed Barb. "So much for peaceful, quiet thoughts in the high mountains!"

The tension burst, and everyone laughed, including Steve, who said warmly, "Barb, what are you taking home with you?"

Barb leaned back in her chair, smiled and said, "I am going to take back many lessons from all of you, but the most important lessons will probably be those that I relearned from the young people here at the ranch.......It's one thing to intellectually accept leadership responsibilities as a CEO or CFO. It really is something else to live it!......It's like smelling coffee the first thing in the morning to listen to Marianne, Gina, Lone Eagle and the other young people talk about how they live and work on the ranch, and to hear the commitment and the work ethic reflected in their words and actions! Phrases stick in my mind come from their hearts so naturally and matter of factly!..... 'Out here, its what you do that counts.'......'Nature doesn't punch a clock.'......'I ride for the brand.'......'We do what needs doing.'......'Out here, the only equality that counts, is being equal to the job.'......'I just can't let a cow down.'........'Character is about having a worthwhile set of values, and the courage to live them.'......'It's about keeping your word; not just the letter of your word, but also, the spirit of your word.'......'If a person can't be honest with himself, he can't be honest with others.'......and after all of that and the long days they put in they have a sense of humor and, 'They get paid $40 a day for being smarter than the cows.'"

As Barbara looked around, she saw that everyone's face contained a smile and an introspective look.

Barb concluded by saying, "These young people may not get paid much, but their values, judgements and smarts are world class! As I leave, I am committed to putting more of these values into my life, leadership, and company!"

The warm afternoon air filled the cool porch with a comforting feel as everyone relaxed, and watched the horses graze in the pasture far below.

Wendy decided to share her thoughts, "Earlier this week, I had ambitions to learn how to become a 'rich' Shareowner, rather than the 'poor' Shareowner that I am.......I got many good ideas!......But, as the week progressed, I thought more about the future, and when I did, like many of you, I thought about the future of our children. In our hearts, we all know that Susan is right: we have to use resources more efficiently if we are to leave enough for future generations.......In the context of our discussions, it occurred to me that if we can measure and get people motivated to increase economic value in the form of Enterprise Value, it is possible for us to increase productivity more than the personal computer, the Internet and the Quality Process combined!......The reason is simple!......People will be working on the right things; things which create economic value.......Right now people are spending a large portion of their time arbitraging accounting rules rather than trying to create economic value. **In many cases, the wrong measures are merely causing people to try to do the wrong things more efficiently!......To do the right things, we must measure the right things!** A big step toward getting people to focus on the right things would be to adopt Valuation Statements and Acquisition Valuation Statements similar to those Sam presented........I hope that not only for Shareowners, but for the sake of our children's grandchildren, we can get people to change the paradigm and to measure and create real economic value!"

There were many light whispers, and everyone nodded agreement with Wendy's observation.

Nancy leaned forward and shared her thoughts, "This week was a cornucopia of wonderful experiences and positive thoughts. As I listened to your comments today, and especially to Barb and Wendy's comments, my thoughts turned to our young people. I hope and pray that the selflessness and wisdom that we have seen in the young ranch hands will be adopted more widely, and that we will quickly adopt the ideas on measuring Enterprise Value that will help stretch our resources further into the future. Most of all, I pray that my children will have the integrity to do, and the personal satisfaction which comes from, an honest job, well done!"

Then, in a somewhat teasing tone, Nancy said, "Sam, I think that I have a name for the 'revolution' which springs from adopting measures and incentives based on creating Enterprise Value!"

Playing along, Sam said, "What's that?"

Nancy replied, "The Effectiveness Revolution!"

"Not bad!......Not bad!" said Sam reflectively.

A few more minutes passed, and only the wind whispered.

Sam knew that everyone wanted to hear his thoughts on the week, so he pushed his hat a little further back on his head and said, "I will always be grateful for warm friendship and good conversation. And, the best conversationalists are the good listeners! You guys and gals have been the best!"

After the chuckles subsided, he continued, "As some of us have learned from Lone Eagle, **'reading sign' is the process of deriving 20/20 foresight from 20/20 hindsight!** It's not magic! It is hard work and self-discipline.......As I listen to the heartbeat of the world around us, it is clear that America and other free market economies need to make a leap in productivity and in reestablishing faith in information that makes our capital markets work.......... To accomplish that, we need to have an 'Effectiveness Revolution' that causes people to do the right things, to take actions that create Enterprise Value and to get paid fairly for doing them........The Effectiveness Revolution begins by admitting that alchemy doesn't exist; and, that for society as a whole there is no Philosopher's Stone that turns accounting numbers into cash.......The Effectiveness Revolution is only credible if we admit that the Emperor has no clothes! We must admit that accounting—as it is presently constituted—does not measure creation of economic value. And we must resolve to immediately fix this oversight!......For the purpose of measuring progress in creating economic value, the Valuation Statements, which we have discussed this week, may not be perfect, but they are directionally correct and 95% better than anything that we have right now!"

Sam paused then concluded, "Measuring and motivating creation of Enterprise Value which is the source of Rich Shareowners and 'rich' nations is not going to be easy. It takes hard work, self-discipline and leadership, which are born of character—not politics!........ But **those of us who have been beneficiaries of democratic, free enterprise have a duty to improve it; we have a duty to 'ride for the brand!'"**

Sam smiled and said, "But my most important hope for the week, is that you all had fun, and feel that you learned a little bit more about the values that helped build this country!"

There were many acknowledgements of that sentiment and applause to support it!

During the rest of the afternoon until the dinner bell rang, everyone replenished drinks and returned to their place on the porch to enjoy small talk.......As much as anything, the group seemed to be basking in the confluence of good memories, a beautiful afternoon in the high San Juan Mountains, and the close presence of people who had gone through an ordeal together. Because of their experience together, it was likely that each in their own way would go out and make a difference.

37.

Until We Meet Again!

It was 9 p.m. Saturday evening. Sam stood tall in front of the guests and ranch hands. His back was to a crackling fire in the giant fireplace of the Lodge Gathering Room. He spoke on behalf of the <u>ST</u> Ranch hands.

"We hope that each of you have enjoyed this brief stay with us!
Each of us is better for our time together.
But, now, it's time to move on.

Some have said that change is the only constant in life.

With poetic license, I will say that even change is not constant!
The rate of change keeps changing.

There are few perfect answers, but there are often practical answers.
The cowboy knew that all answers whether perfect or practical had
to live up to a standard.
The distance of his times make it difficult for us to see his precise
standards. ....We would like to believe that the values conveyed by

Hopalong Cassidy, Roy Rogers, Gene Autry and the Lone Ranger represent those standards.

We do know that cowboying was a rough life!
Riding the vast loneliness of the plains, herding cows around the clock, enduring nature and overcoming man, the cowboy had to constantly adapt to survive.

But through it all, he had to have learned humility, a sense of himself in the universe, and a sense of fair play. He surely learned how to laugh at himself, and he gained the quiet confidence and pride that comes from a tough job well done!

From these experiences, the American Cowboy became a legendary and heroic figure. His legacy is a standard of conduct to which most of us would aspire;
a standard that includes the characteristics of courage, persistence, honesty, integrity, compassion, true friendship, 'riding for the brand', and doing an honest day's work for an honest day's pay.

I wish you well in achieving these qualities in your life!

Thank you for visiting, and we look forward to seeing you again!"

As the guests and hands circulated, exchanging friendship, hugs and kisses, the fire crackled, and in the background, the voices of Roy Rogers, the King of the Cowboys, and Dale Evans, the Queen of the West, softly sang:

'Happy trails to you, until we meet again!'"

Epilogue

As Sunday morning dawned, Wendy left the <u>ST</u> Ranch and drove east on the switchback road, down through trees. She felt the fresh wind in her hair, and lightness in her mind that comes of solving a heavy problem.

She was reminded that most things are pretty simple, when you get rid of the clutter surrounding daily life.......

......Einstein knew it when he wrote $E = mc^2$.

......Shareowners know it when they accept the fact that economic value is created only when they earn more than the cost of their capital.......EP = NOPAT—(Capital x WACC)......

She reflected that there is no alchemy that turns accounting numbers into either gold...or cash!

She did feel deprived that she never got to ask Sam what the 'ST' in the ST Bar Ranch name stood for.......Knowing Sam, she surmised that it probably stood for something like 'Straight *Talk!*'"

But most importantly, she felt that out of this vacation, she had gained some special friends,...and she knew that they would stay in touch......and meet again!

Cast of Characters

Ranch Hands:

Terry Brandon	Trail Cook	Illinois
John Chisholm	Ramrod	Texas
Gina Evans	Wrangler	Midwest
Sean Lone Eagle	Trail Scout	South Dakota
Sam McAllen	Chief Host & Trail Boss	Midwest
Glen O'Rourke	Wrangler	Midwest
Dakota Smith	Head Wrangler	Belle Fourche, S.D.
Jan Wilmoth	Office Manager, Chief of Greeting, Cooking & Cleaning	Colorado
Marianne Robertson	Wrangler & Head Drover	Midwest

Guests:

Wendy Stevens	Searcher and Investment Banker	New York, NY
Jose & Maria Mendoza	Jose: Founder, Owner of $400mm Manufacturing Business; Maria: Homemaker	Michigan
Debra & John Morgan	Debra: Professor Northwestern University School of Business; John: Attorney Children: Nicholas, Cassandra and Lauren	Evanston, Il
Nancy & Steve Patterson	Nancy: Chemical Engineer Steve: CFO of Billion dollar high tech firm Children: Emma, Fletcher	Boston, Mass.
Patty & Jim Perrier	Patty: HomemakerJim: Stock BrokerChildren: Paige, Alexa and Jack	Atlanta, Ga.
Susan & Ed Rogers	Susan: Manager, Environmental Protection Agency Ed: Equity Analyst in a major bank	Charlotte, S.C.
Georgia & Tom Roman	Husband & Wife long distance truck driving team	Washington state.
Barb & Mitch Thompson	Barb: CEO, $5 billion public consumer products company. Mitch: Vice President, Human Resources at a different, large consumer products company.	Midwest

Bibliography

- Hans Christian Andersen, *The Emperor's New Clothes* (www.geoc-ities.com)

- Aristotle, *The Nicomachean Ethics* (Amherst: Prometheus Books, 1987)

- Tom Brown, Jr., *The Way of the Scout* (New York: The Berkley Publishing Group, 1995)

- Peter Drucker, *The Effective Executive* (New York: Harper & Row, 1967)

- Al Ehrbar, *EVA: The Real Key to Creating Wealth* (New York: John Wiley & Sons, Inc., 1998)

- Will James, *Pragmatism* (Cleveland: Meridian Books, 1969)

- Eliyahu M. Goldratt, *The GOAL: A Process of Ongoing Improvement* (Great Barrington: The North River Press, 1992)

- Louis L'Amour, *Trouble Shooter* (New York: Bantam Books, 1994)

- William Manns & Elizabeth Clair Flood, *Cowboys and Trappings of the Old West* (Santa Fe: Zon International Publishing Company, 1997)

- Kent Nerburn, *The Wisdom of the Native Americans* (Novato: New World Library, 1999)

- Thomas Paine, *Common Sense* (New York: Penguin Books, 1987)

- Mary Pope Osborne, *American Tall Tales* (New York: Alfred A Knopf, 1991)

- Alfred Rappaport, *Creating Shareholder Value* (New York: The Free Press, 1998)
- Robert Slater, *Jack Welch and the GE Way* (New York: McGraw-Hill, 1999)
- Brian Sterling, *The Best of Will Rogers* (New York: Crown Publishers, Inc., 1979)
- G. Bennett Stewart, III, *The Quest for Value: The EVA™ Management Guide* (New York: Harper Business, 1991)
- Don Worcester, *The Chisholm Trail: High Road of the Cattle Kingdom* (New York: Indian Head Books, 1994)

About the Author

Will Marshall has over 27 years of experience in corporate finance and as a corporate officer. In 2000 he retired as Treasurer of Nalco Chemical Company, a $2.5 billion, global water treatment company. Upon becoming Nalco's Treasurer at age 34, he built and managed a world class, global Treasury operation for over 20 years. He served on the Boards of a number of Nalco's international subsidiaries, including those in India, Saudi Arabia and Canada. He has been invited to speak on financial topics at insurance and bank forums in addition to training Nalco's managers worldwide. Will began his career in international banking and worked in the Seoul Korea branch of The First National Bank of Chicago (now Bank One).

Will and his wife, Bev, built, own and operate The Meadows Farm Ltd., a hunter/ jumper and dressage training facility in Hawthorn Woods, Illinois.

Will is a 1968 graduate of Lehigh University with a BS in Industrial Engineering, *cum laude*. He did 2 years of graduate work at the Wharton Graduate School of the University of Pennsylvania. In 1985 he completed the Advanced Management Program at Harvard Business School.

From 1970–1974, Will served as a Lieutenant, Naval Flight Officer and Mission Commander in the US Navy.

Will is an Eagle Scout, and in 1999 was named a Distinguished Eagle Scout.

The author can be contacted at www.will-marshall.com.

0-595-21789-3